Cincinnati Day

Tiny Journeys from
The Queen City

Jennifer Renee Reed

Schiffer
Publishing Ltd

4880 Lower Valley Road, Atglen, Pennsylvania 19310

Other Schiffer Books on Related Subjects:

Cincinnati Ghosts, 978-0-7643-2899-2, $14.99

Greetings from Cincinnati, 0-7643-2561-2, $24.95

Greetings from Ohio: Vintage Postcards 1900-1960s, 0-7643-1711-3, $14.95

Designed by "Sue"
Type set in Souvenir

ISBN: 978-0-7643-3716-1
Printed in China

Schiffer Books are available at special discounts for bulk purchases for sales promotions or premiums. Special editions, including personalized covers, corporate imprints, and excerpts can be created in large quantities for special needs. For more information contact the publisher:

Published by Schiffer Publishing Ltd.
4880 Lower Valley Road
Atglen, PA 19310
Phone: (610) 593-1777; Fax: (610) 593-2002
E-mail: Info@schifferbooks.com

For the largest selection of fine reference books on this and related subjects, please visit our website at:
www.schifferbooks.com
We are always looking for people to write books on new and related subjects. If you have an idea for a book please contact us at the above address.

This book may be purchased from the publisher.
Include $5.00 for shipping.
Please try your bookstore first.
You may write for a free catalog.

In Europe, Schiffer books are distributed by
Bushwood Books
6 Marksbury Ave.
Kew Gardens
Surrey TW9 4JF England
Phone: 44 (0) 20 8392 8585; Fax: 44 (0) 20 8392 9876
E-mail: info@bushwoodbooks.co.uk
Website: www.bushwoodbooks.co.uk

Contents

Dedication

I dedicate this book to...

• My parents, Jeff and Karen Phillips, who first opened my eyes not only to the wealth of entertainment and knowledge to be discovered in my native Buckeye State, but also to so many other things. It is because of you I have not only the thirst to seek what the world has to offer, but also the contentment with what immediately surrounds me. I wouldn't trade our little road trips for a million beach vacations.

• My grandmother, Arleen Givens, to whom I owe my love of nature. She taught me how to walk in the woods without disturbing the vegetation or making a sound — by placing my heel down gently and slowly resting the ball on the ground with each step. She showed me the soft moss where deer bedded down to stay cool and taught me never to pick all of any one kind of flower so it would always be able to replenish itself. Her lesson about jewelweed as an antidote to poison ivy has come in handy more than once.

• My brothers, Ryan and Josh, my partners in crime. Though we'd often cringe at the suggestion we were going somewhere "educational," deep down we secretly loved these places as children and appreciate the memories we share.

• Lastly, to my husband Neil, my travel buddy, voice of reason, history buff, and best of all, my companion for all of my journeys to come.

Acknowledgments

Thank you to...

Nate and Stacia Burke~ Don Keating ~ Terry and Becky McClain ~ Jim Flavin ~ Mike and Carol Reed ~ Brad King ~ Tim Scheurer ~ Mark Mirabello ~ Jeanne Halladay ~ Larry Henry ~ William H. Brock ~ Terry Driapsa ~ Breanne Spetnagel ~ Robert Forrey

Introduction

Tiny Journeys

Growing up and living in Cincinnati, it's pretty easy to find something to do. With a world-class zoo, fantastic art galleries, and museums chock-full of interesting displays and special events, The Queen City boasts a lot for its diminutive size.

If you have grown tired of your surroundings, there are plenty of diversions in the surrounding cities — from sporting events to outlet malls and amusement parks.

There are those cabin fever-fueled weekends and warm summer nights, though, that call for exploration and a trip off the beaten path. Major attractions such as theme parks and shopping centers have their place, but there are many tiny journeys to be had.

When I was growing up, my parents took my two brothers and me to the areas surrounding Greater Cincinnati to explore the rich history and offbeat attractions that are often omitted from travel guides. If we were short on funds and long on time, we'd drive aimlessly — but we'd often find plenty of interesting places to stop along the way. We traipsed through our state parks, testing our skills in identifying the flora and fauna our grandmother taught us about.

Instead of simply checking out a book about Ulysses S. Grant, my parents took us to see his birthplace, making history come alive. I remember standing at Rankin House, an important Underground Railroad stop, as a young girl. I stared down from the top of that tall hill and looked to the Ohio River, imaging the feat that was crossing it to safety and freedom. After visiting Serpent Mound in Adams County, I strived to learn more about our Native American history and became interested in archeology.

I recall hunting fossils, picking up buckeyes, and breaking open walnuts that would stain my hands. I played in the heavy native clay, forming crooked pots and rustic beads and hardening them in a campfire like the objects I'd seen that had been plucked from earthworks and put on display.

I love to stand atop one of Southern Ohio's many overlooks, gazing across the Ohio River to Kentucky. I'm always humbled by the thought that not so long ago, slaves risked it all to set foot on Ohio soil and into the safe houses that still stand today, dotting the riverscape in small towns and hiding their honorable secrets.

If I imagine hard enough on a hot August day that I am in a Kentucky cave, I am instantly cooled. I can smell limestone and feel lake water. The whoosh of air and the scent of lemon cleanser upon entering state park visitor centers is a small pleasure. Every chance I get, I sign a guestbook and become one visitor in a long line before and after me. I always look through the pages to see who has come the farthest to appreciate a local treasure and feel honored that a region I call home holds so much value.

Today, as an adult, my memories of childhood in this region are rich and dimensional, but for as many places as I have visited and researched in my twenty-seven years, I have so many more to discover just miles from home.

Too many children are being deprived of the natural wonders of our state, cooped up inside in front of video games or the television. Too many adults living in Cincinnati are unaware of local history and have passed by important historical locations in favor of bigger, brighter, more modern distractions.

Though our family day trips cost little more than the cost of a tank of gas, I truly believe we had just as much fun, if not more, than the kids who went to the beach every year. It is in this spirit of adventuresome, thrifty fun that can be had on a moment's notice that I wrote this guide. Most attractions are in Ohio, though you will find some in Kentucky, Indiana, and West Virginia. At the time I write this, there is no attraction in this book that will cost you more than $25 per person, and many are free. All can be visited by traveling no more than a day's time, most within three hours of Cincinnati. You will learn something from every place you visit. While I do not claim to be a historian, I have provided a short background for each attraction and enough information to get you started — I hope you will be inspired to learn more about these places and delve deeper into their history, significance and opportunities. The chapters cover places I've found to be interesting, but they are not comprehensive by any means — there is plenty more to explore in each area.

So, keep this book in your car or your bag in case you find yourself in need of a place for which getting there is half the fun.

Chapter One

Getting Ready

The author with the road trip essentials she never leaves home without: camera, GPS, notebook and maps. *Used with permission by Neysa Ruhl Photography.*

The best part about this guide is that these trips do not require weeks of planning or, for the most part, not even an overnight bag. However, with a few supplies kept in the car and a few things to keep in mind, these local attractions can be even more enjoyable. Most are common sense, but a reminder never hurts. If you plan on taking off quite often, consider investing in a car organizer that fits in your trunk or behind a seat. That way, you can keep your supplies organized in one place.

Like all good Cincinnatians, I measure trips in minutes and hours, not miles. Most attractions in this book are easily visited in half a day, while others are best suited for an overnight stay. If you're willing to leave Cincinnati early, head back late and plan carefully, even the attractions that are three or four hours away are manageable in one day if you plan well.

What to Take

- Comfortable shoes and socks
- Inexpensive poncho for each person
- Change for donation boxes… It's always a nice gesture to support inexpensive or free attractions
- Moist wipes, paper towels, and bath towels
- First aid kit
- GPS*
- Car chargers for cell phones and GPS devices*
- A good old-fashioned road atlas
- A pen and notepad for sketching plants or animals for identification or to write down things you'd like to look up later

- Sunscreen and Insect repellent
- Cash… Even if an attraction typically accepts credit and debit cards, there is always the chance that the machines will be down — something you don't want to risk with places that are miles from an ATM.
- Compass
- Tissues
- Camera… Make sure you have a full battery and don't forget your card or film. Double check!
- Trash bags… Since 2009, Ohio State Parks have asked visitors to bring their own trash bags in an effort to save money at many parks.

Tips and Tricks

- Call ahead… Many attractions in this book have hours that change seasonally. In addition, low-budget websites aren't always updated right away, so a quick call before heading out is wise.
- Dress for the weather… If you find yourself dressed inappropriately but still want to head out to one of these attractions on a whim, at least make sure you have comfortable shoes.
- Don't count on your cell phone… Many places covered in this book are outside of coverage areas or have spotty service
- Know when to visit… If you're trying to avoid crowds, don't visit on days with special events such as open houses. If you d on't mind crowds, those days may be the best deal for your money. Sometimes holidays are the best time to visit outdoor attractions such as parks; many are rarely crowded on major holidays (especially during winter months) and it gives you a chance to burn off all those extra calories from big meals. For attractions that are busier on holidays, such as State Parks, call the attraction to ask about "off" weekends, which often occur the week before or after a holiday.
- Know your limits… Most of the attractions in this book are accessible to people of all ages and ability levels; however, there may be some trails that are best left to advanced hikers or climbers. Most park maps or websites will specify trail ability levels and distances.
- Use common sense when visiting secluded, wild areas… For instance, rocks are slippery after it has rained, poisonous snakes live in the region, and the weather changes quickly. Pay attention, stay alert, and take a friend! Don't touch or disturb wildlife and leave things as you found them.
- Know your limits, part 2… If you find yourself out late and become tired, stop! Drowsy driving is dangerous. The cost of a cheap hotel is tiny compared to your safety. If you don't mind heading out in the same clothes you had on the day before, you can even hit a few attractions on the way home!
- Where to eat… Even if you plan to stop for meals, take some healthy snacks and water just in case. Brochures located at hotels and in rest areas often contain coupons for restaurants and attractions, so make a stop when you're near your destination.

- Confirm tour hours... If you're visiting a cave, call ahead to confirm they are open for tours. A recent spread of white-nose syndrome, a fungus that is harmful to bats, has closed some regional caves.
- *Lastly, VERY IMPORTANT... NEVER leave valuables in the car, even if you're parking in an isolated location. Remember that visible cords and mounts can attract thieves.

Other Ideas

- If an attraction is a good spot for an interest of yours, such as caving or bird-watching, contact the site to see if they have any special or private tours available. This is also an excellent idea for birthdays, marriage proposals, or other special events.
- Geocaching is a popular activity involving a handheld GPS. There are many websites and books to get you started in this hobby, which takes you to some very interesting places you might not otherwise visit. Many sites in this book are teeming with caches!
- Be sure to take family photos in front of landmarks such as park signs, rock formations, and other things that will likely be here years from now. People enjoy revisiting the locations seen in the background of their childhood photos.
- Pack a picnic... Dining facilities are indicated in each chapter so you know where to stop for grills, picnic tables, and restroom facilities.
- Contact the attraction in advance if you plan on touring with a large group. Not only is it courteous to other day-trippers, but it's also a great way to get discounted tickets and parking — some places even offer private tours if your group is large enough.
- If you plan on visiting a large cemetery, check online beforehand or with the office when you arrive to see if there are any notable burials of celebrities located there.

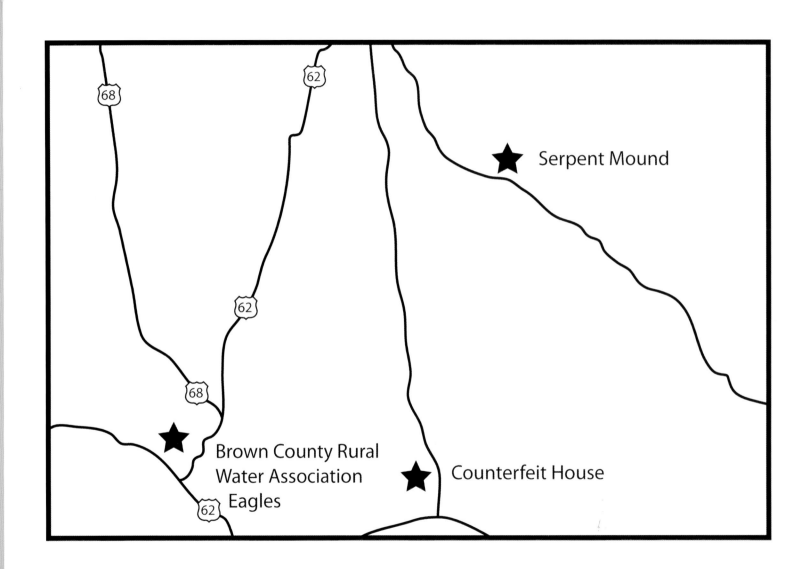

Chapter Two

Appalachian Foothills

Adams and Brown counties perch on the edge of the Appalachian region with people who commute to jobs in bigger towns and cities and farmers who work the land. This area mixes the old and new, stitched by State Route 32 into a crazy quilt of local legend, ghost stories, tradition, and prehistory.

It's often tempting to head out to the country as soon as the feeling of urban claustrophobia creeps in. With its sprawling soybean and cornfields, punctuated only by the occasional crow, it's the perfect place to stretch your legs and enjoy the outdoors.

Driving a little slow on a back road, occasionally moving to the side to let a combine pass, will get you a thankful finger lifted from a wheel in a tiny wave so familiar in the area or a slow, deliberate nod of the head. Attempt that in Cincinnati traffic, and you might get a different sort of gesture.

Languid summer days were meant for the country. Pungent animal smells are somehow comforting. As the land rolls by in gentle hills, it's easy to feel like you sit at the feet of giants. In fact, the Appalachian Mountains find their roots here, in the foothills.

It's the proud history and preservation of old ways that make Adams and Brown counties such fascinating places of escape.

Serpent Mound

3850 State Route 73, Peebles, OH 45660

- **Hours**: Memorial Day weekend – Labor Day
- **Cost**: Personal Vehicle $7.00, Motorcycles $2.00, RV or Commercial Van $9.00, School Bus $35.00, Commercial Bus $70.00

Serpent Mound, located in Adams County, Ohio, is mysterious for many reasons. Like Stonehenge, part of the allure is that nobody quite knows what it's purpose is or was. Also like Stonehenge, it could have had religious, supernatural, funerary or astronomic purposes. In fact, the structure and

placement of the mound does seem to match up rather well to locations of heavenly bodies on significant dates.

When my husband and I visited the British Museum in 2003, we found artifacts from this mound and a small display about its history. It was odd to find something so under-appreciated here to be celebrated in one of the world's great museum collections.

This is not a burial mound, though two (or more) are located nearby. In addition to its cryptic purpose, legend has it a large black panther, obviously not indigenous to Ohio, is spotted by locals. The marker reads:

> One of North America's most spectacular effigy mounds, Serpent Mound is a gigantic earthen sculpture representative of a snake. Built on a spur of rock overlooking Ohio Brush Creek around 1000 A.D. by the Fort Ancient culture,

the earthwork was likely a place of ceremonies dedicated to a powerful serpent spirit. The site is located on the edge of a massive crater, possibly formed by the impact of a small asteroid around 300 million years ago. Frederic Ward Putnam studied Serpent Mound between 1886 and 1889. Due largely to his efforts, Serpent Mound became the first privately funded archaeological preserve in the United States.

People who enjoy history with a dose of mystery will be intrigued by Serpent Mound. A visit here is a great way to get kids interested in history and appreciation for Native American culture. Bring your binoculars to scan the fantastic view and be sure to visit the small but informative museum located in the visitor's center for the history of the Fort Ancient people.

Brown County Rural Water Association Eagles

3818 US Highway 52, Ripley, OH 45167

- **Phone**: 937-375-4106
- **Hours**: Viewing area open seasonally during daylight hours; contact for more information.
- **Cost**: Free

Sure, you can view eagles at our world-class Cincinnati Zoo, but did you know that some have taken up roost in their natural environment just over an hour outside of the city?

Since 2005, American Bald Eagles have been nesting in a protected area on the grounds of the Brown County Rural

Opposite page: Serpent Mound

Water Association near Higginsport. Beginning in late winter when the eggs typically hatch, small crowds gather in the area near the Brown County Rural Water Association. Though the association built an observation area that was heavily used for years, the eagles have since moved to a more private nesting area. Their offspring can be spotted in White Oak Creek fishing in the late winter and early spring; the mature nesting pair can also be spotted.

Wildlife lovers and photography buffs will enjoy this destination, perfect for a spur-of-the-moment get-out-of-the-house trip. Bring a pair of binoculars, your telephoto camera lens and watch for one parent hunting for food while the other guards the nest.

Opposite page: An immature bald eagle near White Oak Creek.

Counterfeit House

Gift Ridge Road, Manchester, OH, 45144

- **Phone**: 937-544-5454
- **Hours**: Always visible from the street, but please respect that this is on private property
- **Website**: http://www.adamscountytravel.org/history.html

The Counterfeit House, hinted at only by small handmade signs on the side of the road, has a sordid history and fascinating secrets.

Dating back to 1840, this Adams County attraction served as headquarters for a major counterfeit money operation. Bills and coins produced here were circulated among riverboats. This is a house of tricks — there are false locks, hidden compartments in doors for the plates used to produce bills, and legitimate chimneys piped smoke through to false ones that gave the appearance of normalcy to rooms used for the illegal deeds.

Unfortunately, the privately owned Counterfeit House was damaged in a 2009 winter storm and needs repair, so there are currently no regular tours. However, the interesting house is viewable from the road. If you'd like to help save this piece of history, please contact the Adams County Visitor's Bureau.

Counterfeit House

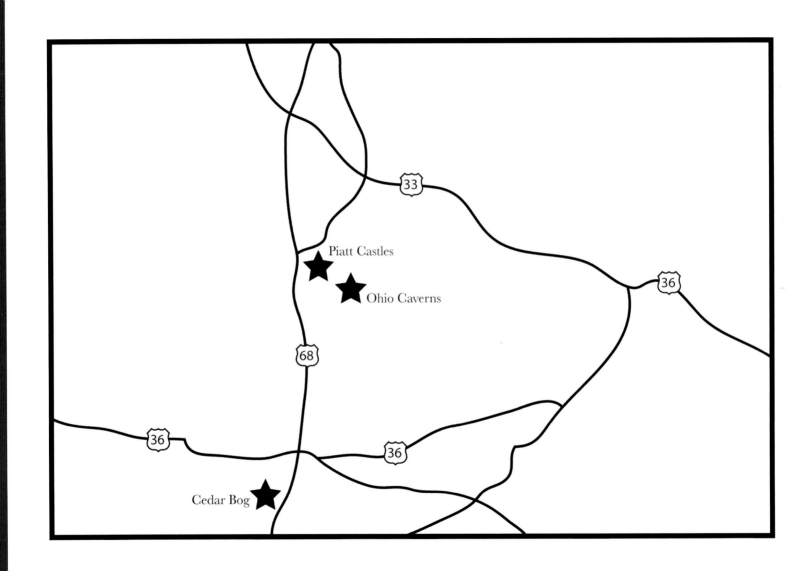

Chapter Three

Unusual Ohio

I'm often struck by how often Ohio comes up in movies and literature as a bland, generic setting. If your character isn't a fast-paced New Yorker or a sunburned Southern California surfer, it seems best to hail from the Buckeye State, which evidently serves as a blank backdrop for story development.

What these novelists and screenwriters fail to realize is that Ohio is hiding some spectacular gems. While much of the state does admittedly look the same, it would be a shame to let these out-of-the-way places pass by your window (or underneath you!) because you didn't find it worth your time to stop and explore.

Sure, we have stretches of highway that will make you sick of seeing corn, but our great state also boasts eight presidents, the world's longest wooden coaster, America's first traffic light, is the birthplace of the first man to walk on the moon, the birthplace of aviation, the first lighted nighttime professional baseball game, and has the only pennant-shaped flag out of any state. Not a bad list by any means. The attractions in this chapter highlight a nifty part of the Buckeye State that definitely deserves some attention, if not a spot on this impressive list.

Cedar Bog

980 Woodburn Road, Urbana, OH 43078

- **Directions**: Drive four miles on south US Route 68 and then west on Woodburn Road for 1 mile to signed entrance and parking lot
- **Phone**: 800-860-0147
- **Hours**: Wednesday-Sunday, 9 a.m. to 4 p.m.; may vary seasonally
- **Cost**: $4.00 per adult and $3.00 per student; if no one is at the kiosk, please leave your money in the blue box.
- **Website**: www.cedarbog.org

Cedar Bog

Located just an hour and a half from downtown Cincinnati, Cedar Bog is unusual in every respect. To begin, this unique moist, cool environment is technically a fen, which is fed by a natural spring. A second rarity is that it is rarely crowded, even on fair spring days. Thirdly, you will see and hear things in this out-of-the-way park you won't encounter anywhere else in Ohio, including rare orchids and nearly fifty plant and ten animal species that are either rare or endangered in our state (Ohio Historical Society, 1999).

The fragile, balanced environment plays hosts to a variety of amphibians and birds, and trout flourish in Cedar Run, the stream that feeds this fantastic fen. Visitors are treated to a boardwalk that loops through the park, allowing them to enjoy the experience without muddy feet or disturbing the fragile wildlife. There is even one point where visitors can step off the boardwalk and jump on the spongy ground!

There are times when the stillness is almost unbelievable. The moist air, heady with the scent of mosses and black soil, is permeated occasionally with birdsong or the chirp of a frog. Such delicately beautiful flora and fauna inhabit this place that it doesn't take a huge leap for one to imagine they've taken a deep nap and awoken to a land made for sprites.

If you are so lucky as to visit this magical microcosm, please treat it as though it really were a land plucked from a fairytale. This little gem — a murky emerald in Ohio's jewel case — is a treasure indeed.

Located about an hour and a half away, Cedar Bog is well worth the trip for the unique flora and fauna. Plus, the fact that it is somewhat isolated means that visitors often find they are the only ones there. Perfect for families with older children, nature buffs, orchid hunters and photographers, this preserve is a peaceful place to reflect on Ohio's beauty.

Make sure you wear shoes with good traction as the boardwalk gets wet and slippery with moss, binoculars, and a plant and an animal guidebook. Watch for skunk cabbages in February (check the website for special events such as the February Skunk Cabbage Walk or Boo at the Bog in October) and showy yellow ladyslippers in June.

Piatt Castles

10051 Township Road 47, West Liberty, Ohio 43357-0497

- **Phone**: 937-465-2821
- **Hours**: Hours vary seasonally, so please call for more information.
- **Cost**: Adults: $12 for one castle, $20 for both; Children: $7 for one, $12 for both; Seniors (65 and older) and AAA Members: $11 for one, $18 for both.
- **Website**: www.piattcastles.org

Delightful in every way, the Piatt Castles maintain the perfect blend of preservation and delicious decay.

The houses of the Piatt brothers, Abram and Donn, stand in silent witness to the surrounding hills and the animals that roam them. Inside Mac-o-Chee, the frozen eyes of a taxidermied owl look over the still home and its eclectic furniture and wonderfully creepy corridors.

Popular as wedding sites, the two homes, Mac-o-Chee and Mac-o-Cheek, are silently jolly. For as large as each structure is, the personalities of each are barely contained by stone walls. In some places, nature has reclaimed parts of the houses, giving them an effect Frank Lloyd Wright would approve of.

Though Wright might smile at the blending of nature and dwelling, he would almost certainly disapprove at the ornate, exaggerated, Gothic architecture. After paying a small fee at the chosen house, a tour guide will begin on the ground floor of each home by informing visitors of the home's past. When this introduction is complete, visitors are free to traipse through the houses, peek into rooms and sometimes look back over their shoulders because it seems these places must be haunted.

Though the houses are well-cared for and are being renovated as this is being written, the peeling paint and squeaky floorboards evoke a certain romance that is lost in most preserved historic homes. Admiring a mural, faded with time, in late afternoon light spilling

Opposite page: Piatt Castles

through a rain streaked window would make Jane Eyre proud.

The castles are located about two hours from Cincinnati and are in close proximity to Ohio Caverns. Architecture and history buffs will be especially delighted with a visit here, though there are plenty of surprises for the kids (look for the ghost in Mac-o-Chee!) and plenty of great photo opportunities for shutterbugs.

Ohio Caverns

2210 East State Route 245, West Liberty, OH 43357

- **Phone**: 937-465-4017
- **Hours**: April 1-October 31, 9-5; November 1-March 31, 9-4.
- **Tours**: Regular: Adults, $12.50; Children 5-12, $7.00; Historic: Adults, $18.50, Children 5-12, $12.50; Children 4 and under, free.
- **Website**: www.ohiocaverns.com

Ohio's largest cave system, Ohio Caverns, is a family-friendly attraction that is comfortable year-round. Boasting a constant temperature of fifty-four degrees year-round, the clean, moist environment is a cool oasis in the summer and a warm getaway for those with cabin fever in colder months.

Generally, cave tours are good bets for families with children looking for a fun, safe, and educational experience. Armed with a few rules (don't wander off and don't touch the delicate cave walls or formations), visitors can purchase timed tickets in the modern, spacious gift shop and join the tour of their choice. The grand finale of the Regular Tour is the Palace of the Gods — sure to wow young and old alike. The knowledgeable tour guides truly enjoy their jobs and happily take questions. (There is also an Historic Tour, which is an extension of the Regular Tour and takes visitors to parts of cave that were open from 1897-1925.) While video is not allowed, visitors can take still photographs.

It takes approximately two hours to get to West Liberty, Ohio, where the caverns are located. When combined with the other attractions in this chapter, this is a long day-trip or a nice weekend trip if you'd like to spread out your stops a bit. Allow at least two to three hours at the caverns; picnic areas are located on the grounds if you'd like to take lunch.

Perfect for just about anyone, this particular system of caves is great for first-timers and has a nice souvenir shop and a reasonably priced gemstone mining sluice experience that's perfect for kids.

Comfortable walking shoes are a must, as well as dressing in layers. Also bringing a change of socks and shoes is advisable — remember caves are often damp!

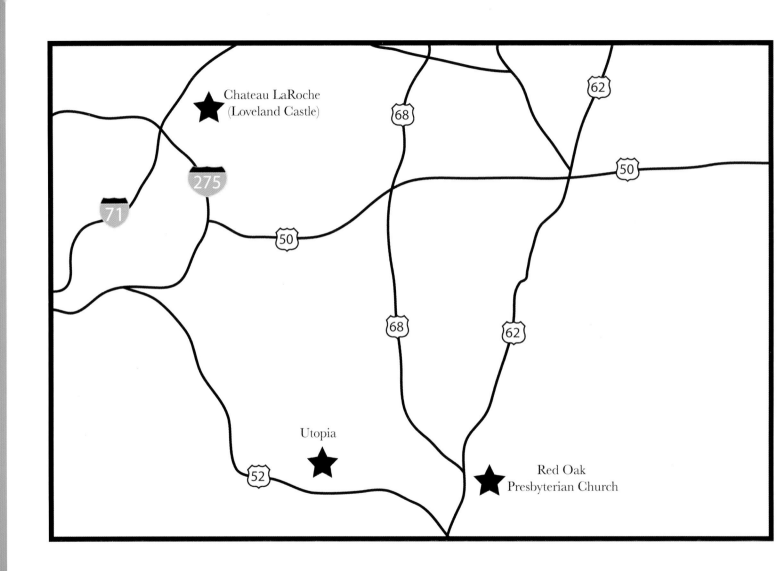

Chapter Four

Colorful Characters and Local Legends

With so many sleepy towns steeped in history, Southern Ohio is home to many local legends and ghost stories. Sometimes the stories behind the rumors are even more intriguing than the rumors themselves.

Unlike most chapters in this guide, this one details three attractions located in different areas for a mini-tour of fascinating people and places. With the right timing, it is possible to visit these three locations in a day or weekend.

Utopia

No Address — Private Property

• **Directions**: Take Kellogg Road/ US-52 East toward New Richmond. Continue to follow US-52. It is near the Clermont-Brown County line.
• **Hours**: Visible from the road during daylight hours; there's an historic marker you can read.

From the road, Utopia doesn't look like much. With a population smaller than some college classes and the quiet sensibility that comes with sleepy river towns, it's easy to ignore, but if you've passed the convenience store, you've also passed a very important and odd piece of Ohio history.

Right next to a small carryout you will see a small clump of plants and trees around a chain-link fence. What's inside this fence on, or more accurately under, private property is a piece of history hidden from the unknowing eye.

The story begins in 1844, when followers of the French philosopher Charles Fourier decided to seek a new start. The founders attempted to revive their idea of a perfect society after disbanding the ill-fated Clermont Phalanx. This place they would call Utopia offered them a new start. They believed in community and cooperation and depended on trade from Cincinnati for supplies. The fee to live in Utopia was $25. The original plat map, which is on file at the Clermont Historical Society, shows a neatly designed row of equal-sized pieces of land. The aged, hand-penned technical drawing tells nothing of the interesting beliefs held by the members or the tragedy that would befall future residents.

The residents of the Fourier sect believed that humankind was perched

Opposite page: Utopia

on the edge of a 35,000-year period of peace and perfection. Famously, they also believed that the salty oceans would turn into lemonade, since the most perfect thing an ocean could be was a source of drinkable, delightful liquid.

After the oceans remained mere saltwater and the small settlement faced financial and social problems, the community was disbanded. The land was later sold to John O. Wattles, a Spiritualist who also sought many of the same communal goals as his predecessor on the land. The community, under the direction of Wattles, built an underground church with vaulted ceilings and dual entrances, so that the members could practice their religion without fear of reprisal or suspicion from locals, though climbing underground to attend religious services surely raised some eyebrows.

At some point, the revived community decided to move the town hall built by the Fourier followers. Going against the knowing voices of local residents, the Spiritualists moved the hall brick by brick down to the edge of the Ohio River. Just barely finished, the residents threw a party

on the evening of December 13, 1847. Already swollen from melted ice and snow, the Ohio flooded and broke through the south wall of the building, sweeping residents and their guests out into the icy night. Most died of hypothermia or drowned in the racing waters. Several people survived, including Wattles and his brother, who were not at the hall at the time of the flood. They moved elsewhere, though a few remained as late at the 1870s. According to local legend, the ghosts, most often in a group of three, appear in soaked clothing at the doors of local homes and to people who find themselves near the site of the tragedy late at night.

Unfortunately, the most famous landmark (the doomed hall's foundation is now underwater) visible today, the underground church, is on private property and closed to the public. However, you can stop to see the new Ohio Historical Marker and maybe buy a pop from the carryout, which stands only yards from the church's entrance. If you find yourself driving through after dark or on a cold, wet winter night, keep

your eyes peeled — you just might spot one of the infamous dripping-wet spirits that reportedly haunt the area.

Aunt Jemima's Grave

5754 Cemetery Road, Ripley, OH 45167

Located just over an hour from Cincinnati is the Red Oak Presbyterian Church and Cemetery. While the older tombstones are interesting to read and the surrounding woods envelop the property in a mantle of privacy, many people who visit the cemetery are not there for the scenery. They can't help but turn off the highway after seeing the church sign that announces it as the final resting place of Aunt Jemima.

According to the Northern Kentucky University, Rosa Washington Riles, a Red Oak resident, was recruited by the Quaker Oats company to dress as Aunt Jemima:

Aunt Jemima's Grave

You may not recognize the name Rosa Washington Riles, but you probably recognize Aunt Jemima, the name of the character she portrayed. Riles was born in 1901 in Red Oak, Ohio, a small farming community located fifty miles east of Cincinnati. In her mid-30s, Riles left Red Oak to work for the Quaker Oats Company. Quaker Oats hoped to bolster the public's interest in their self-rising pancake mix by bringing their trademark to life. During the Depression, major newspapers carried Help Wanted Ads, seeking several dozen attractive black women to dress as Aunt Jemima and travel the nation,

giving cooking demonstrations with Quaker Oats' self-rising pancake mix (Sroufe, 2004).

While it's easy to see why the Aunt Jemima brand has changed the stereotypical image of black women since Riles's time, there is still a sense of pride in the area for the brush with fame achieved by a woman from Red Oak. Her grave is located in the new section of the cemetery.

Loveland Castle

12025 Shore Road, Loveland, OH 45140

- **Phone**: 513-683-4686
- **Hours**: Open daily, 11 a.m. to 5 p.m., April through September; open weekends, October through March (Call to verify times)
- **Cost**: $3 per person
- **Website**: www.lovelandcastle.com

Loveland Castle

Though I've traveled Europe and seen many great castles, one of my favorites is in my own backyard. Loved by locals for its quirkiness, Chateau LaRoche, or as it is better know, Loveland Castle, perches on a piece of land overlooking the Little Miami at the bottom of a steep, winding road built by the same man who single-handedly built the entire castle: the eccentric genius Sir Harry Andrews.

Andrews was a fascinating man who met an untimely end. He had an inventor's mind and constantly tinkered with contraptions and eventually built the castle out of bricks he made using milk cartons and crushed cans.

The plot of land where the castle sits was donated by the parents of two Boy Scouts who received the land for the bargain price of a year's subscription to the *Cincinnati Enquirer*. Sir Andrews decided that his Boy Scout Troop needed a place to conduct their meetings, so he built a scale model of a castle using cement, milk cartons, dirt, and rocks. Unfortunately, Andrews died at age ninety-one after being badly burned at the castle and suffering from gangrene.

Today, the castle is stuffed to the gills with artifacts and antique furniture. A walk around the castle grounds turns up beautiful gardens and imaginative stone structures reminiscent of European grottos. In warmer months, canoes and kayaks glide by; in fact, you may even arrive by watercraft to visit or picnic.

The group that protects the castle to this day, The Knights of the Golden Trail, began as Sir Andrews's troop. Today, the Knights give tours and answer any questions. Of course, like any good castle you may visit, there are ghosts — just ask any Knight for the story.

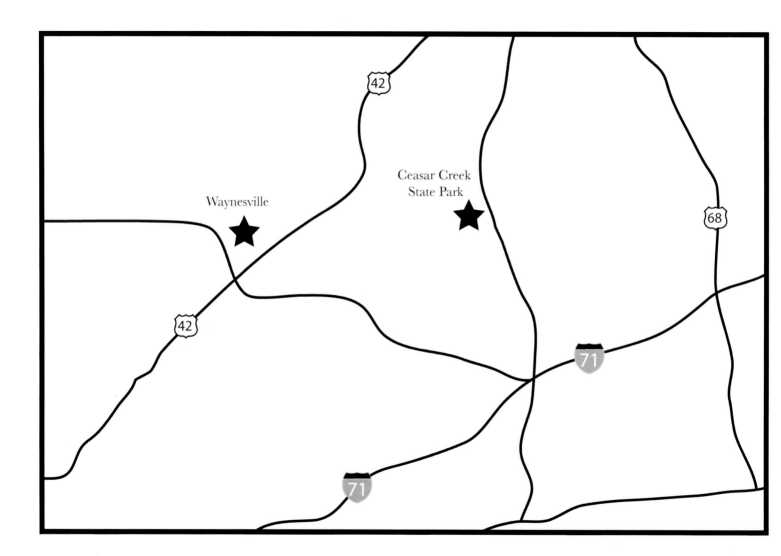

Chapter Five

Waynesville

With candy and ice cream shops, arts and crafts boutiques, and high-quality antique stores, Waynesville is a perfect way to spend a lazy Saturday. The shops are odd in that charming way — beautiful merchandise in renovated buildings where the age shows through despite the best efforts to cover it up. The colorful rows of storefronts display bright flags and potted plants without a trace of irony — you see, Waynesville is not only known as the Antiques Capital of Ohio, it's known as the Ghost Capital too.

As is the case with many old Ohio towns, the concentration of spooky stories may be attributed to the sheer amount of colorful characters, settlers, and military troops that have passed through the area. Being perched near the Little Miami River and a stop on the

Waynesville

Little Miami Railroad, there certainly must have been a constant influx of visitors — not all of them up to good. Today, you can visit several buildings that claim to be haunted, including the Stetson House, which offers tours.

If you are willing to brave the ghosts for some great shopping, remember to

take cash (many accept debit and credit cards, but there are always exceptions), reusable shopping bags, and your holiday shopping lists. Most shops are located on or around Main Street, so it's quite easy to park somewhere and walk. Better yet, combine your trip with the Sauerkraut Festival, held each year during the second weekend of October and get a head start on Christmas season purchases.

Be sure to also visit Caesar Creek State Park, a local favorite popular for its recreational opportunities, and then top off your day with a visit to Der Dutchman, a popular restaurant and meeting place with a country-style menu sure to build your strength back up after shopping or hiking.

Stetson House

234 South Main Street, Waynesville, OH 45068

• **Hours**: Wednesday to Saturday, 12-5 p.m.
• **Cost**: Free to visit the store, but for a donation of a few dollars, you can ask for a tour.
• **Website**: TrendyBindisBoutique. com (this is for the store that occupies the building)

Waynesville's Stetson House is currently a cute boutique filled with trinkets, jewelry, and retro goods — not exactly where you'd expect to find ghosts milling about. However, a few things allude to the house's history: a historical plaque near the door shows its designation as a historical property and a hand-written sign on the door offers ghosts tours.

John Stetson, widely known as the producer of the ten-gallon Stetson hat, visited his sister Louisa at this house. Unfortunately, John's visit led to the demise of his sister — he spread tuberculosis to her and she died from the disease in 1879. People claim to smell gingerbread despite the fact that the house does not have a kitchen anymore. Louisa's ghost has been seen, dressed in dark clothing. Also, there are mirrors that don't stay on the walls!

Stetson House

Caesar Creek State Park

8570 East State Route 73, Waynesville, OH 45068

- **Phone**: 513-897-3055
- **Hours**: Daily, 6 a.m. to 11 p.m.
- **Cost**: Free
- **Web**: www.caesarcreekstatepark. com

Caesar Creek is popular destination due to its public beach, bass fishing, 2,830-acre lake, trails, and picnic areas. Visitors can also explore a village with fifteen reproduction buildings that demonstrate how people lived in pioneer times.

Caesar Creek Gorge State Nature Preserve is located on park grounds and is home to important geological features such as the gorge formed from glacial waters. The creek empties into the Little Miami, making it important to protect the land and keep it clean.

Located just miles from Waynesville, it also serves as a stopover location for those in town for shopping, festivals, and other events.

Ceasar Creek

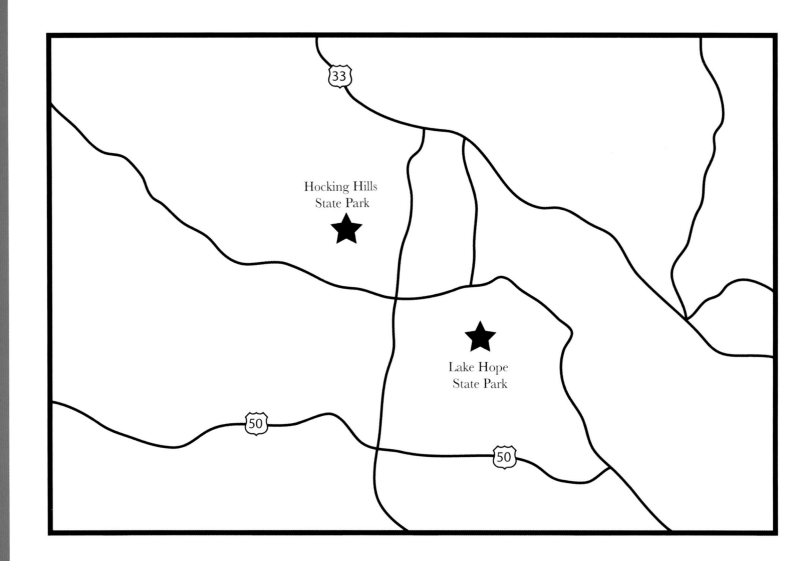

Chapter Six

Head for the Hills

How much time must pass before we regard carved graffiti as historic rather than with disdain? I saw some from the 1980s and it seemed to mar the rock surface, but another inscription from 1809 fascinated me. Is the difference that the features of Hocking Hills were once just part of a larger wilderness, something that was expendable since so much of the country was still uninhabited? Is it that old human instinct to mark something not everyone could find? Now that we have fewer and fewer of these beauty spots to visit, they have become more valuable and there isn't the need to claim where you have been — since so many have been there before. Perhaps that instinct to commemorate a visit still lingers, even when it no longer means anything.

The human touch is what both worries and intrigues me about this beautiful region. It's a great place to visit and it's worth taking better care of. Fortunately for us, it is well maintained and efforts are underway in some areas to restore the natural landscape.

Hocking Hills State Park

19852 State Route 664 South, Logan, OH 43138

- **Phone**: 740-385-6842
- **Hours**: Opens a half-hour before sunrise, closes a half hour before sunset.
- **Cost**: Free
- **Website**: www.dnr.state.oh.us/parks/tabid/743/Default.aspx

Hocking Hills is full of evidence of the human urge to leave a mark, as the graffiti demonstrates.

The interesting thing about the graffiti is that many tour guides and historians will point out old examples, usually from the 1800s, but will also ask that people refrain from adding to it. While this is totally understandable, I think it's worth noting that the only difference between the graffiti pointed out by tour guides and that which is discouraged by them is age.

Carving into rocks destroys them over time, but the carvings also serve as a sort of ledger or log. You can see who was where and when, and sometimes even what they were doing. Teens who carved names and dates into Rock House in 1890 probably did not get into trouble since those areas were not protected at that time; teens who do the same in 1990 would have been kicked out of the park or worse.

This beautiful park is comprised of six basic areas: Old Man's Cave, Ash Cave, Cedar Falls, Conkles Hollow, Cantwell Cliffs, and Rock Shelter. Each area offers unique beauty and unforgettable landscapes.

While many people from Cincinnati head to Hocking Hills for long weekends, visiting this beautiful area is doable as a day-trip if you are willing to get up early. For those who want to stay longer, this is an area rich in accommodating innkeepers and cabin owners.

Hocking Hills

Hocking Hills is located about three hours from Cincinnati. While an overnight stay in a cabin, campground, or nearby hotel will allow visitors to take their time visiting various areas of the park, choosing only one or two places is advisable for a day-trip.

People of all ages can enjoy the park, though some trails are more accessible for children, the elderly, or those with limited mobility than others are.

Be mindful of snakes (including the copperhead), deer on back roads, bear (rare but possible), and natural hazards such as slippery rocks and steep cliffs. While the trails are well marked and safe, being mindful of your footing and keeping children nearby is advisable. Also, Old Man's Cave is supposed to be haunted by the ghost of its namesake, so listen carefully when you visit.

Because it's tough to know which caves will be busy, I will provide some guidance here, but I have grouped all of them into one stop — that way if one is busy, you can visit another.

Try visiting Old Man's Cave early in the morning before it fills with tourists, as this is easily the most popular site. During peak times, try Cantwell Cliffs or Rock House, two of the more out-of-the way caves. For an easy hike, head to Ash Cave, which is manageable even when energy reserves are low.

Please be respectful of the environment and other hikers. Unfortunately, there are too many people who leave trash or let their children climb on delicate rock formations and swim in ponds where signs clearly state not to do so. Please remember the old saying: "Take nothing but pictures, leave nothing but footprints."

Lake Hope State Park

27331 State Route 278, McArthur, OH 45651

- **Phone**: 740-596-5253
- **Hours**: Daily, 6 a.m. to 11 p.m.
- **Cost**: Free
- **Website**: www.lakehopestatepark. com

This tube of nectar allows visitors to feed the hummingbirds at Lake Hope.

Like the Jackson Lake region mentioned in *Chapter Fifteen*, the Lake Hope State Park land was once heavily logged for timber to fuel the Hope Furnace during the days of a booming iron industry. What you will see today is second-growth forest with abundant wildlife, including beavers that build dams in small inlets at the lake (Ohio Department of Natural Resources, 2007). Today, remnants of the furnace remain, though the new forest has reclaimed the area and covered many traces of what occurred over one hundred years ago. In addition to the furnace site, visitors can also enjoy a full-service campground, water sports, fishing, lake swimming, and miles of trails. The park is entirely surrounded by the Zaleski State Forest.

In recent years, Lake Hope has received a lot of attention for their hummingbird feeding program, a story which has been picked up by many local, state, and national publications. From June to August (check the park's website for days and times), visitors may try hand-feeding hummingbirds at the park's visitor's center. Each person gets a small tube of nectar with a pipe cleaner handle. With a little patience, you may be one of the lucky ones who get a tiny visitor.

A naturalist is on hand to teach participants about the nimble creatures and the Lake Hope State Park Hummingbird Oath: "I promise to clean and fill my feeders daily." This rule ensures the health of the hummingbirds and keeps them coming back. This program is great for people of all ages, including children — just remember that you must be quiet and still! It's quite easy to spend an hour or more at just this event. Remember to visit inside the visitor's center for information on local wildlife and to pick up a park map and, if you are going to try your hand feeding the hummingbirds, please consider leaving/making a donation to the center.

Moonville Tunnel

Lake Hope State Park, off of Shea Road

- **Phone**: 740-596-5253
- **Hours**: Daily, 6 a.m. to 11 p.m.
- **Cost**: Free

Wherever you travel, if you find yourself around a campfire telling ghost stories, some classics are bound to come up: a crybaby bridge, a ghost that will appear if you flash your headlights, a lady in white staring wistfully out a window waiting for her lover. While these stories are often given a local twist, there is typically little to no truth to the supposed events behind them.

That's why the Moonville Tunnel located at Lake Hope State Park is so fascinating — there is physical evidence to back up the premise of the horror story that accompanies it. There is plenty in the factual history to suggest eerie activity could take place if it were to

This tunnel is allegedly hunted, so BEWARE!

happen at all—whether you believe in the supernatural or not.

While visiting Lake Hope State Park, I happened to pick up a historical tour brochure and discovered that the Moonville Tunnel was on park property. (The brochure gives turn-by-turn directions.) On one of my many visits to the Forgotten Ohio website, this story caught my eye and I made a mental note to visit one day. Because I have planned many trips to weird spots, it was funny to happen upon this

local gem by accident, as I had always assumed the Moonville Tunnel was something you weren't encouraged to visit and thought it was on private property. Much to the contrary, the park maintains a road and trail, and a forest ranger keeps an eye on things since copperheads abound.

On our visit, a kindly park ranger acted as gatekeeper, giving us the choice between a creek crossing and a poison ivy-riddled path that would surely end in days of itching. We chose wet feet. While the tunnel is supposed to be haunted by a drunkard who fell on the tracks one night and was killed, we saw no signs of ghosts. We did, however, see plenty of messages left by past visitors.

This place is prime for ghost hunters (obey park hours), railroad enthusiasts, explorers of abandoned structures, and college students. This site is *not* recommended for small children. Also, watch out for poison ivy, copperheads, and high water at creek crossing — it sounds scary, but with a little care, you'll enjoy your visit.

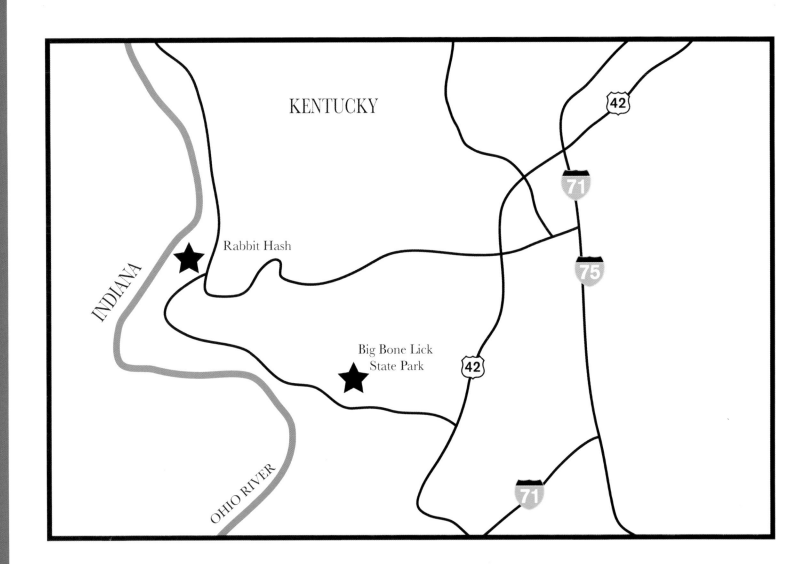

Chapter Seven

Northern Kentucky

Many Northern Kentuckians are very clear about one thing — they are not from Cincinnati. This assertion is less about anything being wrong with the city and more about the sense of pride for Northern Kentucky's unique attractions and way of life found in the area just south of the river.

While Cincinnati gets much of the attention with gorgeous Eden Park, shiny new sports stadiums, and fine dining, Northern Kentucky has much to offer in the way of history that was often overshadowed by The Queen City's booming industries and importance as a port of call on the Ohio.

It takes less than an hour to travel to Big Bone Lick and Rabbit Hash, where you can learn to appreciate two very different aspects of Northern Kentucky's history.

Big Bone Lick State Park

3380 Beaver Road, Union, KY 41091

- **Phone**: 859-384-3522
- **Hours**: Daylight hours
- **Cost**: Free
- **Website**: www.parks.ky.gov

Tread the same grounds explored by Lewis and Clark — and before them, mammoth herds, stag-moose, and other prehistoric creatures. Home to a new interpretive center that displays the big bones of animals that met their fate in the park's boggy ground and salt licks and gave the park its name, Big Bone Lick is an excellent introduction to the importance of the area in archeological history.

While Native Americans had spoke of prehistoric animal remains for years, it wasn't until the 1700s that explorers and traders made official record of their discoveries and gave us much of the information we have today. According to the journal of explorer Robert McAfee, the area near the salt springs were chock-full of mammoth bones, which were apparently used by his men as chairs and tent posts. Delaware Indians told McAfee that the bones had been there for as long as their people could remember (*History of Big Bone Lick State Park*, 2009).

In 1803, Meriwether Lewis visited Big Bone Lick, sending fossils and notes to President Thomas Jefferson. William Clark visited on Jefferson's request in 1807 and collected more specimens.

Big Bone Lick State Park

Today, the park is a family-friendly 525-acre recreation area, complete with a campground, visitor's center, sports facilities, and trails. The American Buffalo herd is accessible by a level trail and is popular with children and photographers. It's a nod to the past of the Northern Kentucky area — where buffalo roamed freely until the early 1800s.

Make sure to visit in October, when the park puts on its annual Salt Festival, complete with salt harvesting demonstrations, lye soap making, historical encampments, and period weapons demonstrations.

Rabbit Hash

**10021 Lower River Road
Rabbit Hash, KY 41005**

- **Phone**: 859-586-7744
- **Hours**: Call for hours
- **Cost**: Free
- **Website**: www.rabbithashusa.com

Since salt was used in those days to preserve food, the area became popular. The forests supplied plenty of wood for fires to heat the water until it boiled down to nothing but salt. Later, in the 1800s, Big Bone Lick became well known as a mineral spring where people believed they could improve their health by bathing in or drinking the water.

Rabbit Hash is one of those places where you either get it or you don't.

A blink-and-you-might-miss-it hamlet perched on the Ohio River bank overlooking a riverboat casino, Rabbit Hash is a far cry from the bells and whistles found only five minutes in any direction. It's a place that embraces quirkiness and an Appalachian sensibility and anachronism. From the honor system shopping at a small "Everything Store" to the Rabbit Hash General Store, whose floor is covered with peanut shells and serves as a home to several critters, this small town doesn't mess around with unnecessary fanciness or shiny gimmicks. In Rabbit Hash, you get what you get.

While it may seem unfriendly to outsiders who visit the General Store, it's evident that this is the turf of a small group of regulars who gather around the stove and discuss the latest happenings — most often without looking up when a tourist comes in. It's alright, as you are welcome to look around.

While the stories behind the town's name vary as much as what the mayor

Rabbit Hash

is paying attention to (P.S. she's a dog), most sources point to eating rabbits during some sort of scarce time, most likely a flood.

Just under an hour from Cincinnati, Rabbit Hash is a magnet for bikers, curiosity seekers, and confused Sunday drivers who took a wrong turn and ended up at the "Center of the Universe," as locals like to call it. Grab some peanuts at the General Store, buy a bumper sticker, and enjoy the enigma that is Rabbit Hash.

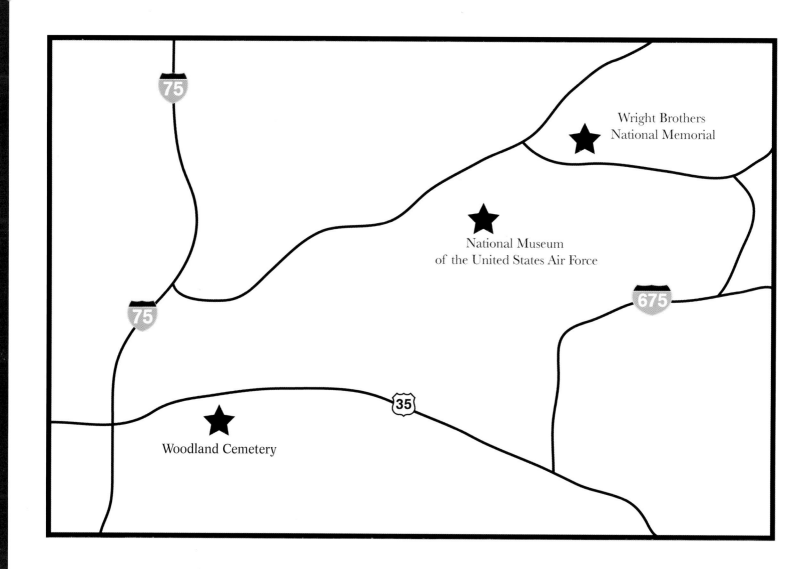

Chapter Eight

Ohio's Aviation History

When I was little, we often went to the Dayton Air Show and to visit the National Museum of the United States Air Force. When I was around the planes, I was always most interested in the nose art — especially that which appears on World War II aircraft because most of it follows the theme of beautiful, curvy bombshells and pinup girls. Despite my feminist upbringing, I appreciate the nostalgic value. I also feel a little sad for the men who missed the women waiting for them back home — many ladies painted on planes were modeled after sweethearts and wives.

While the museum is certainly the showpiece as far as tourist attractions go, there are other aviation-related stops you should add to your itinerary. You may visit the Wright Brothers Memorial, which overlooks Huffman Prairie Flying Field (where the brothers conducted many experiments), and the Wright family plot at the beautiful Woodland Cemetery. It's amazing to see all of these monuments and realize that Ohio is the birthplace of aviation. That's something to be proud of.

In addition to these attractions, Dayton has great shopping, casual dining, and beautiful metro parks. While you're at Woodland Cemetery, Johnny Morehouse (who has nothing to do with aviation) just might steal the show.

National Museum of the United States Air Force

1100 Spaatz Street, Wright-Patterson Air Force Base, Ohio 45433

- **Phone**: 937-255-3286
- **Hours**: Open daily, 9 a.m. to 5 p.m. (closed Thanksgiving, Christmas and New Year's Day)
- **Cost**: Free
- **Website**: www.nationalmuseum. af.mil

Opposite page: WPAFB Museum

Many people have heard of this museum, but it's a place many have yet to visit. There's a perception that unless you're an aviation buff you will be bored, which could not be further from the truth. People of all ages get a kick out of old war birds, interpretive exhibits, and the interesting tours. It's not a bad place for ghost hunters, either.

Two of my favorite planes at the museum are a B17 Flying Fortress called the Shoo Shoo Shoo Baby after a popular song and a B24 called the Strawberry Bitch. The latter, along with several other planes in the museum, is rumored to be haunted.

Even if you know next to nothing about planes or aviation history, a trip to Dayton is an excellent way to spend a day or two. The museum is huge — we were there for six hours on our last visit — and there is now a Presidential and R&D tour (these are very popular, so get there early).

Woodland Cemetery and Arboretum

118 Woodland Avenue, Dayton, OH 45409

- **Phone**: 937-228-3221
- **Hours**: Daylight
- **Cost**: Free
- **Website**: www.woodlandcemetery.org

Located within throwing distance of the University of Dayton, Woodland Cemetery is the final resting place of many famous people, including most notably humorist Erma Bombeck (marked by a large rock near the entrance) and Orville and Wilbur Wright (section 101, lot 2533).

During office hours, visitors may borrow audio equipment and a CD and take an auto tour of the grounds. During the course of the year, several interpretive tours are offered.

A visit to this cemetery is a peaceful, reflective occasion. Surrounded by the

Woodland Cemetery and Arboretum

grandest monuments imaginable and down to the most humble of stones, each grave tells a story. In the spring, new life springs forth in flowering trees and bulbs planted by the living to honor the dead. In the winter, quiet snow falls on the dismal gray stones, reminding one that this is, after all, a place to honor the dead. This silence is broken only occasionally by that Ohio standby — the red male cardinal, belting out his song for nobody in particular.

While the graves of Bombeck and the Wright Brothers garner much of the attention from visitors, the grave of Johnny Morehouse is the stuff of legend.

From Forgotten Ohio

This is the grave of Johnny Morehouse and, according to legend, his dog — and they are Woodland's most famous ghostly residents. The story might be rooted in nothing more than an unusual tombstone, but this is what they say: Johnny fell into the Miami & Erie Canal and froze to death, despite his faithful dog's efforts to pull him out. After he was buried, the dog lay on his gravesite and wouldn't be moved. Eventually it died from starvation and sadness. A special stone was made in 1861 to commemorate the dog's devotion. People leave toys, candy, flowers, and other trinkets on the stone — someone once had even tied a bandanna on the dog's neck. It's a ritual the cemetery management tolerates (*Woodland Cemetery Hauntings*, 2009).

Symbols like this monument are important to perpetuating local legends. I suspect there is some truth to the story, though the Victorian penchant for all things dramatic makes it very likely that there was strong elaboration involved somewhere along the line.

I find it interesting the way in which physical objects with sketchy histories spawn stories that are passed down through the generations. It seems like every small town has a crybaby bridge, haunted cemetery, or a satanic church. A creepy old building, a dangerous intersection, or even an abandoned playground likely has a story attached. The fun part is finding the kernel of truth behind the symbol.

If you would like to visit Johnny and his faithful dog, find section 82, lot 546.

Johnny Morehouse's grave

Wright Brothers Memorial

2380 Memorial Road, Wright-Patterson Air Force Base, OH 45433

- **Phone**: 937-425-0008
- **Hours**: The interpretive center is open daily 8:30 a.m. to 5 p.m. (closed Thanksgiving, Christmas, and New Year's Day)
- **Cost**: Free
- **Website**: www.nps.gov/archive/daav/pla_fac_huffmanprairie.html

No visit to Dayton, Ohio, is complete without a stop at this memorial, located high on a hill across from the Huffman Prairie Interpretive Center. A tall obelisk commemorates the achievements of the Wright Brothers.

Wright Brothers Monument

A path leads down to a paved overlook, from where you can see the Huffman Prairie, the site of many Wright brother experiments.

It's amazing to stand at the overlook and read the signs that detail the Wright Brothers' experiments in aviation — and then look to the Wright-Patterson Air Force Base and realize how far technology has come in the short time since the brothers tinkered with their flying machines. The interpretive center, located at the memorial, offers a gift shop, interesting exhibits, and information about the history of flight.

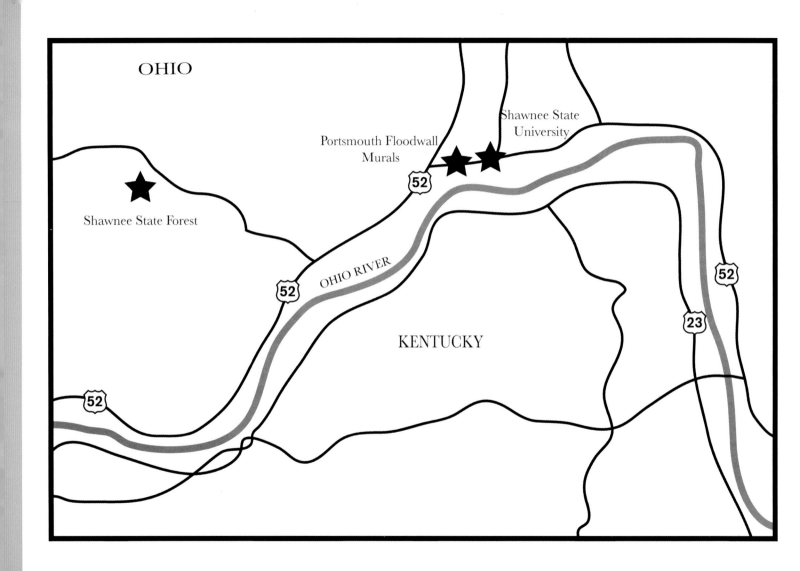

Chapter Nine

Portsmouth

In the interest of full disclosure, Portsmouth holds a special place in my heart. I attended Shawnee State University from 2001-2005, during which I explored the wonderful history, quirky attractions, and old buildings with the man who later became my husband.

On Saturday mornings, we'd get up early (a hard task for college students) and go to Greenlawn Cemetery. There, we'd walk, searching for a rumored witch's grave (which we never found) and read the tombstones of the river town's early inhabitants. After shaking off the early morning dew, we'd head over to the Boneyfiddle district to comb through the antique shops. Many of the results of these treasure hunts are on display in our home today. When we'd satisfied our curiosity on these excursions, we'd head to Ye Olde Lantern for a lazy lunch and then walk back to the campus for an afternoon nap.

Sadly, these days are gone, but a trip back to Portsmouth about once or twice a year takes us back, if only temporarily.

For a town that has sadly seen better days due to industry moving from the area, there is still a sense of pride in its residents. And rightly so — Shawnee State University, a rapidly growing university with successful programs, slowly breathes life into the sleepy town with theater productions, art shows, concerts, and outreach programs.

Professors hailing from all over the United States and the world enrich not only the campus, but also the volunteer activities and committees they are part of off-campus. Interesting architecture, fantastic independent shops, and the Portsmouth Floodwall Murals are happy discoveries for those who find themselves there, and a walk along the Ohio River on a balmy day soothes the mind. Shawnee State Forest, located just outside of town, offers respite for college students celebrating the end of final exams and families looking for a small adventure.

A visit to Portsmouth should include a trip to the Scioto Ribber, a local favorite restaurant that also happens to support the Cincinnati Bengals.

Shawnee State Forest

**13291 US Route 52
West Portsmouth, OH 45663**

- **Phone**: 740-858-6686
- **Hours**: Daily, 6 a.m. to 11 p.m.
- **Cost**: Free
- **Website**: www.dnr.state.oh.us/
Home/forests/ShawneeStateForest/
tabid/5166/Default.aspx

Shawnee State Forest, whose name comes from the Native American tribe, was purchased in 1922. The Civilian Conservation Corps made improvements, adding roads and artificial lakes in the 1930s. Today, it's Ohio's largest state forest and spans more than 60,000 acres. While the sheer vastness of this area may seem daunting, a downloadable auto tour guide is available on the park's website and highlights five major areas for your enjoyment.

Shawnee State Forest — You can hike the trails on foot, horseback, or by AVT. Just be sure to check out conditions and rules before setting out.

Shawnee State University

940 Second Street
Portsmouth, OH 45662

- **Phone**: 740-858-6685
- **Website**: www.shawnee.edu

Shawnee State University is young as far as Ohio's universities go; it was founded in 1986 and started as a branch of Ohio State University. Today it is a four-year college offering over eighty associate's, bachelor's, and master's degrees, a robust sports program, and state-of-the-art classrooms. It is also the proud home of one of only fifty Digistar II planetariums on earth, which is often open for public shows.

A trip to Shawnee State isn't just for prospective students or alumni — most anyone can find enjoyment on the campus. Visit the Vern Riffe Center for the Arts to view the student art that's on display throughout the building. Make sure to check the center's site

Shawnee State University

for upcoming theater events. Head to Clark Memorial Library for a coffee or to browse the three stories of materials — you can even apply for a visiting borrower's card. Sporting events, lectures, and seminars are other great options if you decide to visit.

Portsmouth Floodwall Murals

Located on Front Street

Whenever you see a car driving slowly near the riverside streets of Portsmouth, they are usually looking for the murals. Simply look for Front Street — you'll see the floodwall and about a half-mile of trompe d'loiel murals that depict area history, including Portsmouth Spartan Football, Native American life, Roy Rogers (who grew up in the area), and the industries that built the city in its heyday.

Floodwall

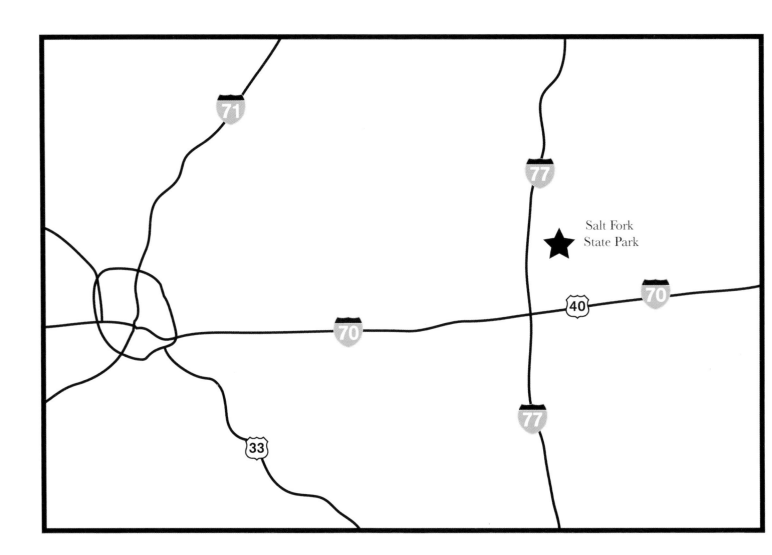

Chapter Ten

Bigfoot in Ohio

When you think of Sasquatch sightings, which locations come to mind? Washington State? Remote Alaskan wilderness? Many Cincinnatians are not aware of a Bigfoot sighting hotspot located about three hours from The Queen City.

Salt Fork State Park

14755 Cadiz Road, Lore City, OH 43755

- **Phone**: 740-439-3521
- **Hours**: Daily 6 a.m. to 11 p.m.
- **Cost**: Free
- **Website**: www.dnr.state.oh.us/parks/saltfork/tabid/785/Default.aspx

When you enter Salt Fork State Park, it might be difficult to imagine it as a hotbed for Bigfoot sightings. After all, this is one of our nicest state parks with miles of immaculate paved roads and a luxurious lodge and golf course. A hotbed it is, though, according to one man.

Bigfoot researcher Don Keating investigates sightings and has been interviewed for countless radio and television shows, including "MonsterQuest" on the History Channel, which dedicated an entire episode to the Ohio Grassman, a Bigfoot-like creature spotted in the Salt Fork State Park region of Eastern Ohio.

According to Keating, the sheer amount of documented sightings and evidence found at Salt Fork has attracted the attention of many researchers — perhaps no piece of evidence more

compelling than the footprints Keating discovered on October 1, 1985.

To add to the convincing nature of many of these sightings and pieces of evidence is the types of people who make the reports. According to Keating, "... some eyewitnesses are professionals in the field they work in. Many eyewitnesses come forward to claim a sighting when they are really putting their career on the line by doing so. They apparently feel very strongly about what they claim to have encountered or they wouldn't step forward, report it and lay their careers on the line by doing so."

So, are you intrigued? If so, head over to the Hosak's Cave area of the park, which Keating reports is a great place to begin exploring. However, Keating cautions, "Go out into the woods to enjoy the woods. Don't go out expecting to find something

This is an actual eyewitness drawing of a creature spotted in the area of Salt Fork State Park (left) on July 2, 1984. The smile or grin on the face was actually observed by the mother who said, "It looked as if it were amused by watching the children on the playground toys at the Grange Hall." *Used with permission of Don Keating, 2009.*

or encounter something. If you do, you are subconsciously setting yourself up for maybe imagining you see something when in reality there is nothing there to begin with. Keep an eye on what is going on all around you. Pay attention to what the wildlife is doing, how it is acting."

In addition to keeping an eye out for Bigfoot, it should be seriously noted that if you choose to venture to Hosak's Cave, you should be very careful. Several serious falls have occurred in this section of the park, including one that was unfortunately fatal. Warning signs

at the trailhead give emergency contact information for this reason; this hike is obviously not for the inexperienced or children. Remember your hiking boots and, of course, your camera — you never know who or what you might run into!

The Museum Scene

If hunting for cryptoids isn't your thing or you need something a little less rough, then head over to the Boyd Glass Museum, the Cambridge Glass Museum, and the Hopalong Cassidy Museum, which are all in the area. While I have not been to these places, I mention them to give you a feel for other things in the area. Also, this is a big art glass production region.

Boyd's Crystal Art Glass

A factory tour allows visitors to witness the creation of beautiful art glass creations and purchase items for their personal collections (including the glass slippers everyone's grandmother seems to own). Located at 1203 Morton Avenue, Cambridge, OH 43725, its hours of operation are 8 a.m. to 4 p.m. Admission is free. For more information, call 740-439-2077.

Cambridge Glass Museum

Opened in 2002, the Cambridge Glass Museum displays fine pieces produced from 1902 to 1958, with over 6,000 pieces to admire. A gift shop, guest activities, and a film round out this experience. In 2008, this attraction was awarded the Eastern Ohio Development Alliance Excellence in Tourism Award. Located at 136 South Ninth Street, Cambridge, OH, its hours of operation are Wednesday to Saturday, 9 a.m. to 4 p.m., and Sundays, noon to 4 p.m., from April to October. For admission rates and more information, call 740-432-4245.

Hopalong Cassidy Museum

Located at South 10th Street, Cambridge, Ohio 43725, its hours of operation are Monday through Saturday, 10 a.m. to 5 p.m. Admission is free. For more information, call 740-439-3967.

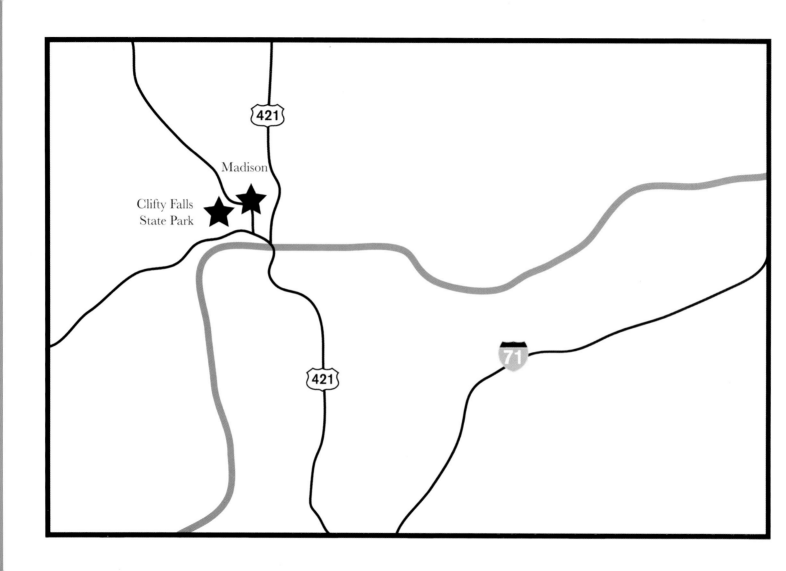

Chapter Eleven

Madison Getaway

It's a joke sometimes heard around Cincinnati that Indiana is the state that is only a half hour away...yet it seems to take three hours to get to.

If you take a scenic route to the quaint town of Madison, Indiana, you may be surprised at how the time flies. The drive from Cincinnati takes about an hour and a half; if you leave in the morning around 8:30, you should arrive just as many of the unique shops are opening.

Known for its nearby park, bed and breakfasts, great shopping and eateries, this little town is the perfect romantic getaway or girls' weekend. I detail three of the main reasons to head to Madison — the wineries, shops, and its close proximity to Clifty Falls — although there are many more things to be found in this charming town. Often overshadowed by

its northern neighbor, Metamora (located about an hour and forty minutes away), Madison is a quieter version, tucked away and waiting to be discovered by first-timers. For information on the places in this chapter, please visit their website at www.visitmadison.org.

Madison Shops

Most shops are on Main and Broad Streets

Upon arrival in Madison, you'll have the urge to park and walk along the delightful streets and duck into each and every little boutique, bookstore, and specialty shop, stopping only for a cup of coffee or some lunch. Whether

Madison bookstore sign

you're shopping for gifts, browsing for the perfect home accent piece, or just looking for a weekend away, people of all ages will find Madison to be an agreeable place.

Suiting all tastes and sensibilities, Madison boasts numerous specialty shops that carry unique items and make for a pleasurable day of shopping. From Churchill's Cigar Shop to Rock-a-Bye Lady, there really is something for everyone. Make sure to check out the Birdhouse Wild Bird and Nature Shop, where you will find everything a budding ornithologist needs and even a hiking trail in the basement. Make sure to stop by the Broadway Fountain. A popular meeting place, the fountain dates back to the late 1800s and was presented to Madison by the Independent Order of Odd Fellows in 1886. It's a great spot to relax with an ice cream cone or coffee and recharge for the rest of your shopping trip.

Madison Wineries

Situated on the Indiana Wine Trail, Madison is the perfect retreat for those who want a day or two with a slower pace to enjoy the small pleasures to be found in quaint family wineries.

Lanthier Winery

123 Mill Street, Madison, IN 47250

- **Phone**: 800-41-WINES
- **Hours**: Tours and tastings are available Wednesdays through Sundays, 11 a.m. to 5 p.m.
- **Website**: www.lanthierwinery

Lanthier Winery is the city's oldest and, according to its website, it has quite a colorful history: "If walls could talk in the old eighteenth century building, they would whisper tales of early trappers and settlers who built the original 24-inch thick stone walls as a haven from the then wild west. What is now the Cellar Tasting Room is believed by some to be an old fort or outpost established by settlers seeking comfort and safety as they moved through uncertain Indian Territory in the mid 1700s."

Thomas Family Winery

208 East Second Street Madison, IN 47250

- **Phone**: 812-273-3755
- **Hours**: Open daily; call ahead for hours, tours, and tastings
- **Website**: www.thomasfamilywinery.us

This friendly winery offers wine tasting, draft cider, tours, board games, and live music on most Saturday evenings — visit its website for more information. Located in a stable and carriage house built in the 1850s, this is a great introduction to Indiana wine and historic architecture.

Madison Vineyards Winery

1456 E. 400 N, Madison, IN 47250

- **Phone**: 888-473-6500
- **Hours**: Open daily, 10 a.m. to 5 p.m.
- **Website**: www.madisonvineyards.com

Also a bed and breakfast, this winery offers tastings, wine gifts, and special events throughout the year, including Twilight Tasting Dinners — four course meals complete with wine pairings. The best part? If you stay at the bed and breakfast, you can taste all the wine you want and not worry about having to drive home!

Clifty Falls

2221 Clifty Drive, Madison, IN 47250

- **Phone**: 812-273-8885
- **Hours**: Daylight
- **Cost**: Free
- **Website**: www.stateparks.com/ clifty_falls.html

If you're ready to put down your shopping bags and tie up your hiking boots, head on over to Clifty Falls, a breathtaking 1,416-acre Indiana State Park that showcases beautiful cliffs, four major waterfalls, and the winding Clifty Creek — a landscape that is a result of the Ice Age.

The Clifty Canyon Nature Preserve lies within the park's boundaries. This area is protected and care should be taken to obey park rules and stay on marked trails to avoid disturbing delicate areas. While popular with hikers year-round, the best time to view the falls is during the winter and spring, when precipitation rates keep them flowing and little to no foliage blocks the view.

If you would like to stay close to Madison and still be close to the natural beauty of this state park, consider a stay in the Clifty Inn, a beautiful full-service inn complete with a restaurant, pool, and gift shop. Camping is also available.

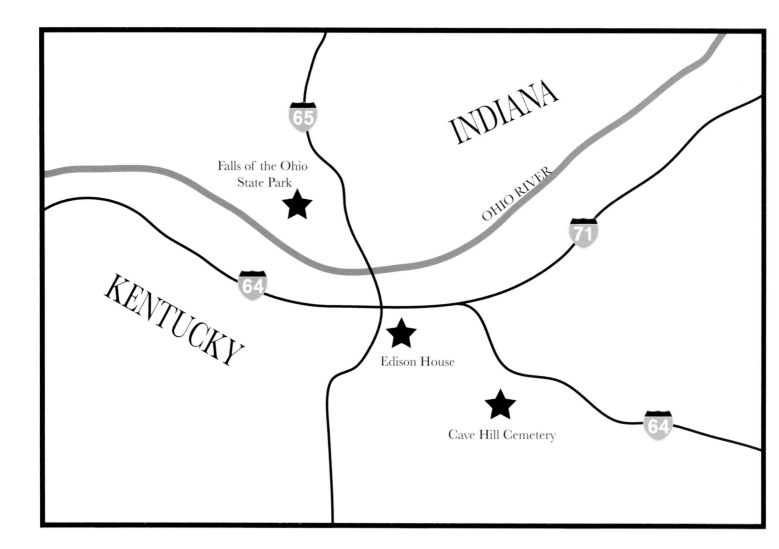

INDIANA

65

Falls of the Ohio
State Park

OHIO RIVER

71

64

KENTUCKY

Edison House

Cave Hill Cemetery

64

Chapter Twelve

Lesser Known Louisville

The city lights of Louisville are exciting. Mixing the flavor of the south with the spirit of a major river city and a fascinating history, this is a great destination for family fun, fine dining, gallery hopping, and shopping. While you would like to travel the hour and a half from Cincinnati to visit major attractions such as the Louisville Slugger Museum and Factory, the Louisville Zoo, or Six Flags Kentucky Kingdom, there are lesser-known attractions that make excellent supplements to the big city fun.

A settlement was first made in the area in 1778 by George Rogers Clark, the older brother of explorer William Clark. The town charter was granted in 1780. The area, specifically the Falls of the Ohio, became very important to America's expansion, as it is where Meriwether Lewis and William Clark laid out the plans for their expedition, which reached all the way to the Pacific Ocean.

Today, Louisville is a modern, exciting city with plenty of diversions. The neighboring Indiana cities of Jeffersonville (named for Thomas Jefferson) and Clarksville (named for George Rogers Clark) see benefit from Louisville's tourism industry as travelers seek the often lower-priced hotels right across the river, still within minutes of the most popular districts.

Falls of the Ohio

201 West Riverside Drive, Clarksville, IN 47129

- **Phone**: 812-280-9970
- **Hours**: Park open daily, 7 a.m. to 11 p.m.; Interpretive Center open Monday-Saturday 9 a.m. to 5 p.m. and Sunday 1 to 5 p.m.
- **Cost**: $2 for parking. If you're visiting the Interpretive Center, parking is free. Monday to Thursday, Adults $4.00 (19 and older), $1.00 ages 3-18, free for children 2 and under. Friday to Sunday and major holidays, Adults $5.00 (19 and older), $1.00 ages 3-18, free for children 2 and under.
- **Website**: www.fallsoftheohio.org

This Indiana State Park is located mere minutes from downtown Louisville, near an industrial area in Clarksville.

The park is located on West Riverside Drive. (Caution to GPS users — there is another West Riverside Drive that will take you almost forty miles out of your way! Make sure you have the correct one before hitting "Go"!) Look for Exit 0 on Interstate 65. Several signs will guide you to the park entrance.

The most important things to know about Falls of the Ohio State Park are: it can be dangerous and requires careful behavior, and that it is illegal to collect fossils and rocks in the park.

Because of the nature of the water flow, currents are swift and dangerous; therefore, there is no swimming and visitors are cautioned to watch their footing on the rock beds along the shore. Children should be carefully supervised and visitors should vacate the rock beds if a flood siren is heard. While this may sound a bit scary, this park is a wonderful excursion and is perfectly safe if rules and regulations are followed.

Falls of the Ohio

While these safety rules seem reasonable enough, some rock hounds and fossil hunters may question the ban on collecting specimens and may not see the harm in taking just one piece. According to the park's website, there's a very simple but important reason for the rule: If everyone did it, there would be nothing left.

For those whose interest is piqued by a walk along the fossil path, the park supplies a limited area where visitors can collect fossils. There are two piles (on my most recent visit they were located near the parking lot in the rear of the Interpretive Center) — Waldren shale and soil — and these are used for the annual Fossil Festival held in September, but in-the-know visitors can search them year-round.

If you're interested, the George Rogers Clark home site is on park premises and is a short distance from the Interpretive Center.

Remember appropriate footwear, as rocks can be slick. Though you can't take fossils from the rock beds home, you could spend hours comparing what you see to a good fossil guide, so if you have one, bring it along!

Cave Hill Cemetery

701 Baxter Avenue, Louisville, KY 40204

- **Phone**: 502-451-5630
- **Hours**: Daylight hours
- **Cost**: Free
- **Website**: www.cavehillcemetery.com

Many Cincinnatians are familiar with the impressive Spring Grove Cemetery and Arboretum.

Cave Hill Cemetery, chartered in 1848, is only a few years younger than Spring Grove, which was established in 1845. Like its Cincinnati counterpart, this cemetery was built in response to the ramshackle, unsanitary burial grounds of the day, which were often so dismal families did not visit the final resting places of loved ones. The opening of these and other park-like cemeteries,

Cave Hill Cemetery

complete with arboretums, gardens, lakes, and fountains, meant that not only could families visit to honor their dead, but also gave people a place to walk and admire the beauty where there was none before.

Located in an industrial part of town, you are instantly transported once you pass through the gates under a stone tower. Visitors drive down a tree-lined avenue, which gently enters the peaceful rows of monuments, nestled among lakes and magnolia trees, which emit a heady fragrance during early summer.

There are several notable burials at Cave Hill: Louisville founder George Rogers Clark (Section P), Harland Sanders of Kentucky Fried Chicken fame (Section 33), and Nicola Marschall, a German-American Confederate sympathizer who designed the Stars and Bars Confederate flag and the grey Confederate army uniform (Section 5, Lot 231).

This peaceful cemetery is best toured by car, as you can drive until a monument interests you — then you simply pull over and explore. Scheduled, guided tours are also available throughout the year; check the website for information.

Thomas Edison House

729-31 E. Washington Street, Louisville, KY 40204

- **Phone**: 502-585-5247
- **Hours**: Tuesday to Saturday, 10 a.m. to 2 p.m.
- **Cost**: Adults, $5.00; 18 and under, $3.00; seniors, $4.00; children under 5 get in for free.
- **Website**: www.historichomes. org/edisonhouse/

Located in the Butchertown district of Louisville in an area near several warehouses, the Thomas Edison House plays a small but important role in Edison's career. This small brick house is nonchalantly tucked between its more modern neighbors. The sign outside the house reads:

… Edison (1847-1931) rented a room in this house. As a young man, he conducted experiments, often all night, then walked to his job as a telegraph operator at 58 West Main Street. Experimenting at work, he spilled acid and was fired. He left Louisville and later developed over 1,000 patents for such devices as photograph and microphone.

While no one can say for sure, perhaps that fateful accident, which led to the end of his employment as a telegraph operator, was just one of the steps that gave us the genius legacy he left behind.

Opposite page: Thomas Edison House

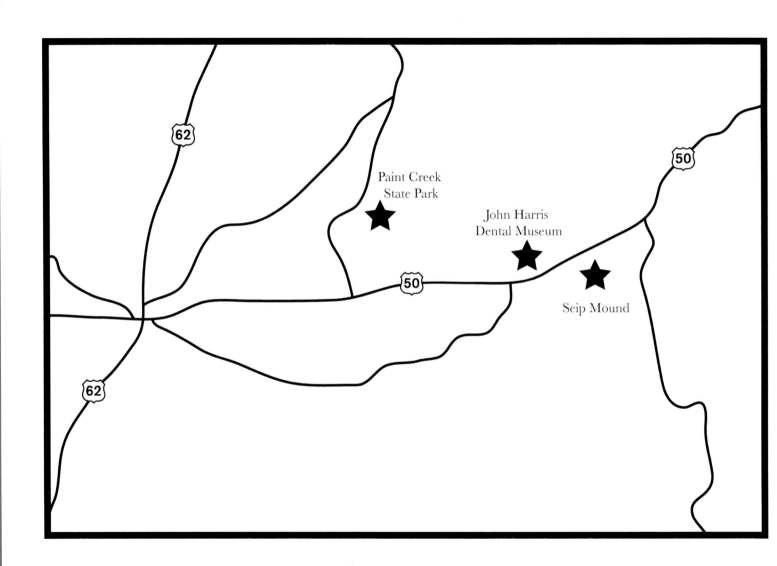

Chapter Thirteen

Paint Creek Region

Paint Creek State Park is located just outside the quaint town and antique shopping hotspot of Bainbridge, Ohio. Just a short jaunt from Cincinnati, this beautiful park offers superb boating, hiking, and wildlife study, as well as one of the nicest campgrounds around. If you're hungry for a good country-style meal, head where the locals go — Bainbridge Timbers, located at 3920 US Highway 50 West, which is close to the park. It's the perfect stop for a hearty meal before or after conquering the many activities you'll find here.

If you're lucky enough to visit Bainbridge during the third weekend of October, you're in for a pleasant surprise. This is when the annual Fall Festival of Leaves is held. Boasting all of the things to love about small-town festivals — music, food, pageants, and crafts — Bainbridge pulls out all the stops and welcomes visitors with open arms. Four scenic loop drives (directions are available at www.fallfestivalofleaves. com), take visitors through some of the most beautiful peak color for miles.

Not coincidentally, Paint Creek State Park is especially beautiful during the autumn months, though a visit or stay is rewarding no matter what season you find yourself in.

Paint Creek

Paint Creek

280 Taylor Road, Bainbridge, OH 45612

- **Phone**: 937-393-4284
- **Hours**: Daily, 6 a.m. to 11 p.m.
- **Cost**: Free
- **Website**: www.dnr.state.oh.us/ parks/paintcrk/tabid/776/Default. aspx

Located about an hour and a half from Cincinnati, this hotspot is for fishermen, cyclists, birders, boaters, canoeists, kayakers, and families with children.

Pack your sunscreen, insect repellent, and binoculars. Serious outdoor gear certainly has its use at Paint Creek, but with some comfortable shoes and a trail map, people of all abilities and experience levels can enjoy a hike. Kids can enjoy several playground areas—and if you decide to stay overnight at the excellent campground, where seasonal scheduled family-friendly activities are commonplace.

As mentioned previously, autumn is an especially popular time for a day trip to the Paint Creek region due to the spectacular fall colors that slowly creep over the hills. Those in-the-know, however, find pleasure in visiting the park year-round and recognize the nuances of each season. Spring brings thawing, of course, and no sooner has the ice melted than fly fishermen can be seen in the early morning sun near the spillway, cracking their lines and donning their waders for the first time of the year. Summer brings the adventurers, ready to tackle hiking and mountain bike trails or take a dip in the cool lake, retiring to tents and campers near the comfort of blazing campfires that beat back the inky night. Winter brings solitude — a near empty campground, snow-covered trails and snapping twigs that reveal wildlife usually kept hidden by thick vegetation.

Like any area with winding roads and desolate stretches of cornfields and old farmhouses, there are a few ghost stories, one of which is the haunting of the New England Club, located in nearby Anderson. It is rumored to be haunted by the ghost of a bride who was left at the altar. Ask a local — you just might get the scoop and have a great story for the campfire.

Dental Museum

209 Main Street, Bainbridge, OH 45612

- **Phone**: 740-634-2228
- **Hours**: Vary seasonally; call ahead for details
- **Cost**: Adults $2.00; children 12 and under free

The John Harris Dental Museum is located in a white brick building in a Bainbridge residential area. Larger than it appears from the street and looking a bit like a tooth perched on a sidewalk lip, this is a fascinating collection of dental tools

Dental Museum

and implement examples spanning the history of the dental profession. Known as the Cradle of Dentistry Education, this former residence of Dr. John Harris, which also served as a dental school, is an important and often overlooked piece of Ohio history.

The long building holds hundreds of false teeth, ceramic ovens for denture-making, a fine example of ivory teeth, as well as fancy dental chairs from the 1800s and enough pedal-operated drills and metal implements to make even the most fearful patient thankful for his or her next modern dental appointment.

Though cases of teeth are to be expected in such a museum's collection, it's still an uncanny effect. Small signs point out interesting pieces in the collection and provide visitors with an overall introduction to dental practice in the 1800s, including an important Queen City connection: fluoride toothpaste was studied and made commercially by scientists at Cincinnati's own Proctor and Gamble. A case containing examples of early commercial dentifrices shows how far products have come since those days; after all, we now have entire aisles of toothpastes, flosses, rinses, and other modern products to keep our smiles healthy and beautiful.

This hour and a half journey from the city is perfect for dental professionals, families with kids, fans of unusual collections, school groups, and college students in dental programs. Though a small admission fee is required, please don't forget some money for the donation box. The little extra money will make you feel good for helping to preserve this little gem.

Don't miss a collection of large ivory and silver toothbrushes and a pediadontist dollhouse cabinet. Check out the pair of ivory teeth on display — and try to imagine how those would feel in your mouth.

Seip Mound

US Route 50 in Ross County

- **Phone:** 614-297-2630
- **Hours**: Daylight hours
- **Cost:** Free
- **Website**: http://ohsweb. ohiohistory.org/places/sw15/index. shtml

Seip Mound is often overshadowed by Fort Hill, a more impressive neighbor

Seip Mound

complete with hiking trails and a small museum. However, don't let the rest stop look fool you. This roadside attraction, located on US Route 50 in Ross County, fourteen miles southwest of Chillicothe and two miles east of Bainbridge, is well worth an hour of exploration.

The central mound is 240 feet long, 130 feet wide, and thirty feet high, with two long, low mounds forming something like a gate as you approach from the parking lot. Other sections were destroyed long ago by agriculture and erosion. The Hopewell tribe used these earthworks as burial sites; there is evidence of a highly advanced society whose members crafted impressive tools and other artifacts, as well as two known structures, marked today by posts and signs.

Allow some time to orient yourself in the small shelter near the parking lot; maps and graphics explain the mound's structure and history, as well as the Hopewell tribe's culture. When we visited in early spring, we were the only ones there for nearly an hour, so take your time and enjoy the peace and quiet.

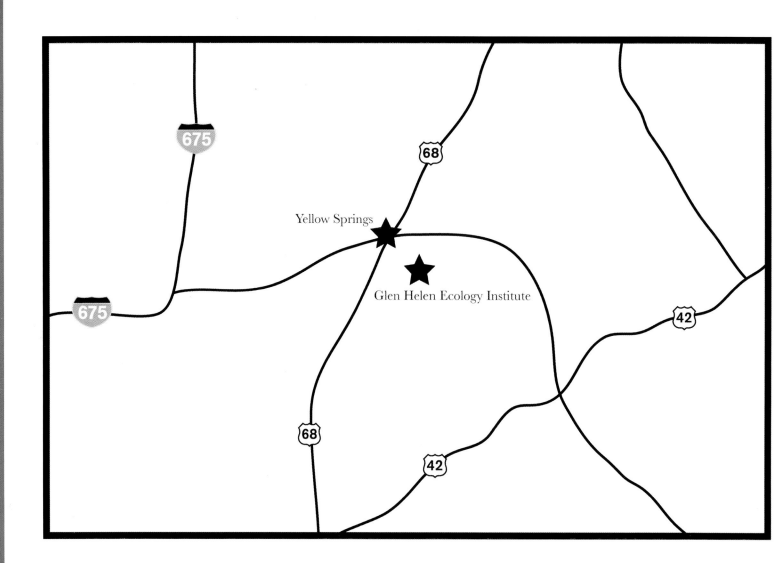

Chapter Fourteen
Yellow Springs

Yellow Springs is an anomaly in Ohio. Rolling cornfields are swapped for eccentric shops hawking earth-friendly goods. Midwest sensibilities are swapped for attitudes normally found in a much more liberal, bigger city. No matter which little shop you step into (and Yellow Springs has dozens), you will be greeted and welcomed with an old-fashioned warmth not often found in today's strip mall-blighted suburbs.

If you have travel to Yellow Springs hoping to grab a bite to eat at a fast-food joint, you're out of luck. While the choice of restaurants is not extensive, they are unique. If you must have a burger-and-fries type of meal, head down to Young's Dairy Farm for a family-friendly dining experience. While the place is best suited for families with small children, folks of all ages can enjoy a good meal for a fair price.

Yellow Springs

A nice introduction to this little town is the bi-annual Street Fair, held in June and October. Featuring hundreds of artists, performers, food vendors, and more, this eclectic event is an excellent opportunity to see many of the shops and brush elbows with the friendly, creative people of Yellow Springs.

Just an hour and twenty minutes outside of Cincinnati, Yellow Springs is a mellow, laid-back town full of intellectuals, college students, artisans, and free spirits. Shopping is a fun mix of art galleries, boutiques, earth-friendly products and head shops. Look for "guerilla knitting" — a friendly type of graffiti created by local artists who knit sleeves onto signs, park bench slats, trees, and just about anything else they can knit around. Local artists Jafra Girls have decorated much of the town, especially near Dayton Street.

Young's Dairy Farm

6880 Springfield-Xenia Road, Yellow Springs, OH 45387

- **Phone**: 937-325-0629
- **Hours**: Vary seasonally; call for details
- **Website**: www.youngsdairy.com

No matter the time of day, Young's will offer you a great menu full of home-style favorites. End your meal with a scoop or two of their famous ice cream, made fresh on the premises. Stop in the gift shop or play a round of miniature golf, but make sure to visit the petting zoo, where you can make friends with many animals including cows, goats, and pigs!

Glen Helen Nature Preserve

**1075 SR 343,
Yellow Springs, OH 45387**

- **Phone**: 937-767-7648
- **Hours**: Open daily
- **Cost**: Free (there may be a small fee for parking)
- **Website**: www.antioch.edu/glenhelen

The Glen Helen Nature Preserve is a wonderful complement to the town of Yellow Springs and Antioch College. With its colorful history and Glen Helen Ecology Institute's dedication to the preservation and stewardship of its natural features, the Glen is a great place to get in touch with Mother Earth and get lost for a few hours. Make sure to visit the spring that gave the town its name (the high iron content means the water's trails are colored a yellow-orange).

In 1924, near where the Grinnell Mill still stands today, two skeletons, which were determined to be Paleo-Indian people, were discovered, likely having been drowned in a bog sometime between 6000-3000 B.C. Evidence has also been found of the Hopewell people, Miami Indians, and the Shawnee. Later, in the early 1800s, the area saw its first white settler, Lewis Davis. Realizing the potential in the area's spring, Davis built a tavern and touted the waters as curing in nature. Later, mills popped up along the Little Miami River and the area became increasingly more settled. The spring's curative properties were still being celebrated and commoditized in the early 1900s (Sanders, 2004).

Today, the Glen Helen Ecology Institute protects this special area and seeks to educate visitors about the unique characteristics worth respecting and taking care of. Remember some sturdy shoes, a picnic lunch, and an open mind — it's the perfect place to unwind.

Be sure to visit the Raptor Center, where injured birds of prey such as owls, hawks, and buzzards are taken for care and the education of the public. Due to the design of the enclosures, it's possible to get very close to these birds without disturbing them. It's a rare opportunity to take a peek at their beautiful feathers and watch their behaviors up close.

Glen Helen Nature Preserve

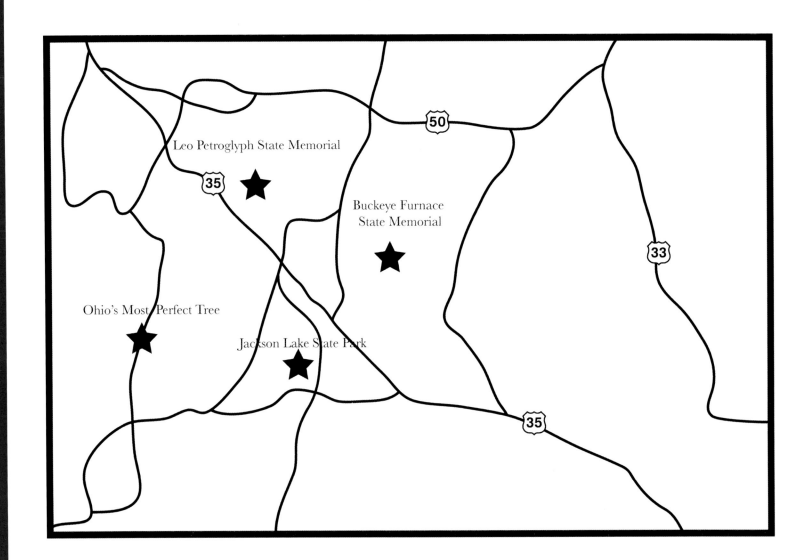

Chapter Fifteen

Jackson Lake Region

Ohio's prehistoric importance is evidenced by numerous limestone fossils, countless Native American earthworks, and beautiful lakes and rock formations carved eons ago. The Jackson Lake region is an excellent example of Ohio's ancient heritage and un-glaciated landscape. Part of the Appalachian Highlands, a long drive in the area will take you through scenic countryside and past Salt Creek, a body of water important to the iron industry that once dominated the area.

Jackson Lake

35 Tommy Been Road
Oak Hill, OH 45656

- **Phone**: 740-682-6197
- **Hours**: Daily, 6 a.m. to 11 p.m.
- **Cost**: Free
- **Website**: www.dnr.state.oh.us/parks/jacksonl/tabid/748/Default.aspx

Jackson Lake sits tucked into the Appalachian Highlands in an area known for its rich prehistoric importance and many varieties of flora and fauna. According to the Department of Natural Resources, the forests visitors enjoy today were once heavily logged to supply the area's iron furnaces (site).

Visitors can enjoy camping, water sports, and fishing. While the park is relatively small and bare-boned in comparison to other state parks, you may avoid some of the crowds you find at more popular locations.

Situated close to Leo Petroglyph State Memorial and Buckeye Iron Furnace State Memorial, Jackson Lake is located almost three hours from Cincinnati and ideally situated for a long day or overnight visit. Remember your fishing pole and take advantage of the bass and muskie populations, among others. The sand beach is a fine substitute if you can't make it to the ocean during the summer.

Buckeye Iron Furnace State Memorial

123 Buckeye Park Road, T-167, Wellston, OH 45692

- **Phone**: 740-978-8021
- **Hours**: Open June to October; Wednesday to Friday by appointment only and Saturday and Sunday from noon to 5 p.m.
- **Cost**: Admission is free for children 5 and under, $3 for children 6-12, $4 for adults, and free to OHS members. The park is free year-round.
- **Website**: www.ohsweb. ohiohistory.org/places/se02/index. shtml

The iron business was booming in the 1850s in Ohio's Hanging Rock Iron Region. As enormous iron ore deposits were discovered in the ground, charcoal furnaces were built to keep up with the new demand for the quality iron that could be produced. Visiting this memorial, which includes a reconstruction of the type of furnace found in the region and a company store that houses a visitor center, is a step back in time to when Ohio was an important player in the iron industry, which lasted for decades.

Located about three hours from Cincinnati, this memorial should be combined with visits to Jackson Lake and Leo Petroglyph for a worthwhile day-trip. Two trails are available on the premises, making this a nice stop for a couple of hours.

Leo Petroglyph

Near the village of Leo, five miles northwest of Jackson, in Jackson County

- **Phone**: 614-297-2630
- **Hours**: Daylight, year-round
- **Cost**: Free
- **Website**: www.ohsweb. ohiohistory.org/places/se05/index. shtml

According to the Ohio Historical Society, Leo Petroglyph contains thirty-seven carvings that depict humans and animals. The Fort Ancient Indians are the likely creators.

The carvings appear on a large piece of sandstone on the edge of a large ravine, making it susceptible to weather and erosion; its isolated location and

Opposite page: Leo Petroglyph

minimal barriers make it a target for vandals who like to add to the ancient carvings. This seems like one of those places you need to see before someone ruins it for everyone.

Nobody knows for sure what the carvings mean, though it appears to be a hunting scene of some sort. Most intriguing is a monster-like horned figure that may represent a shaman or mythical beast.

The small park is also home to a gorge with hiking trails amongst towering sandstone cliff lines and is popular for hikers seeking solitude from the crowds often found at more well-known parks. To get there, turn off of US Route 35 on County Road 28 and then turn left in Leo on Township Road 224.

Ohio's Most Perfect Tree

Ohio's Most Perfect Tree

Route 335, three miles south of Route 32

- **Phone**: 937-365-1935
- **Hours**: Best visited in daylight hours as the hill where it is located is subject to speeding cars
- **Cost**: Free
- **Website**: www.highlandssanctuary.org

Sometimes the best roadside stops are found by chance. Ohio's Most Perfect Tree has no doubt caused countless U-turns and slowed cars — an official-looking sign with white letters bestow this honor on a maple, which is rumored to be over two hundred years old.

Located just three and half miles south of the intersection of Routes 335 and 32 in Pike County, Ohio's Most Perfect Tree stands proudly on the William J. Samson Nature Preserve just outside of Stockdale in the heart of Amish Country. According to Larry Henry, co-founder of the Highlands Nature Preserve, which now owns and protects the tree, it's easy to find. "It's very close to the road which has a small pull off large enough for one car. The little pull-off is easy to miss, so go slowly and watch on the left for a very large Sugar Maple tree."

Located two and a half hours from Cincinnati, this isn't a trip on its own, but if you're in the area and appreciate hyperbole and random roadside attractions, it's worth a stop. Remember your camera — after all, it's not every day you get to meet a tree bestowed with such an honor.

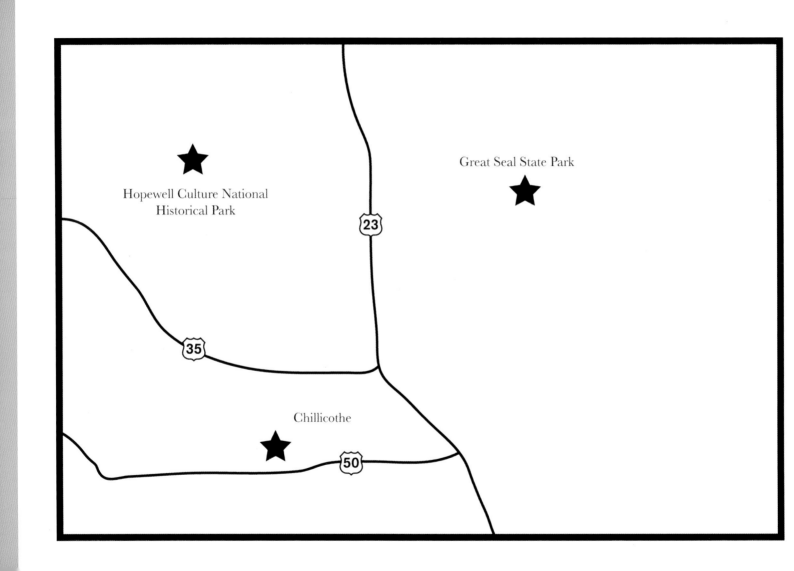

Chapter Sixteen

Ohio's First Capital

Chillicothe served as Ohio's first capital. Nathaniel Massie, whose name can be found in various places all over the region, founded the town in 1796. The town's Native American history, specifically the Adena and Hopewell, is woven throughout, visible as earthworks and evident in park names.

Today, Chillicothe has small-town charm with its primitive and country decor shops, antique stores, and family-friendly parks. The historic district offers fine shopping at favorite stores such as Ivy's Home and Garden, which carries a delightful array of bath and body products, home decor, stationary, and gifts, and The History Store, which offers both fun and functional items representing the Romans all the way up to World War II. The town also offers several bridal salons, making it a

Ohio's first state capital, Chillicothe, is a charming small town to visit and tour.

popular destination for wedding parties. Main and Paint streets are lined with red, white, and blue "open" flags, so be ready to find that perfect gift or a little something for yourself.

While the town is popular among the shopping set, if you're into history, you'll love Chillicothe. Just a short distance from the hubbub of the historic district, you'll find a variety of parks and historical sites that can fill a day on their own. The Chillicothe Paints, a professional baseball team, offers affordable family fun all summer long. If you'd like to stay for a weekend, there is plenty of lodging in town, and several campgrounds and cabin rental companies can be found nearby.

Hopewell Culture National Historical Park

16062 State Route 104
Chillicothe, OH 45601

- **Phone**: 740- 774-1126
- **Hours**: Park open daily during daylight hours; Visitor's Center, 8:30 a.m. to 5 p.m. (Closing time is extended to 6 p.m. Memorial Day to Labor Day.)
- **Cost**: Free
- **Website**: http://www.nps.gov/hocu/

While this park is comprised of several distinct sites, the area known as Mound City and home to the park's visitor's center is perhaps one of the most interesting and impressive places.

Located two miles north of US Route 35 and State Route 104, this park is best conquered beginning with a trip to the interpretive visitor's center.

Hopewell Culture National Historical

Visitors may view artifacts collected in the area, watch a short film, or browse the well-stocked gift shop for a variety of books and souvenirs.

Situated on 120 acres near the Scioto River, there are twenty-three earthworks in the Mound City Group that once served as a ceremonial hub for the Hopewell Culture. Once important ceremonies such as cremations and burials had been performed, the structures where they took place were burned and covered by the earthen mounds. According to the National Park Service, two archeological digs turned up "...objects made of copper, flint, mica and pipestone" (National Park Service, 2008); many of these items are on display in the museum. Since the Hopewell peoples were heavily involved in trading, objects from faraway regions often turn up at these sites as well.

First-time visitors will be simultaneously intrigued and overwhelmed. The mounds come into view from the parking lot, and as you draw closer, their colossal size becomes evident. Several walking trails allow visitors to get up close to the mounds. As you walk amongst these impressive earthworks, remember the importance of this location — the Hopewell peoples would have performed the most significant events and ceremonies of their lives in this very spot.

Great Seal State Park

635 Rocky Road, Chillicothe, OH 45601

- **Phone**: 740-887-4818
- **Hours**: Daily, 6 a.m. to 11 p.m.
- **Cost**: Free
- **Website**: http://www.dnr.state. oh.us/parks/grtseal/tabid/738/ Default.aspx

If you've ever admired the idealistic beauty of the landscape on the Great Seal of Ohio, you'll appreciate a visit to the site that inspired it. According to the Ohio State Parks website:

The park takes its name from the state emblem, "The Great Seal of the State of Ohio." The famous seal depicts a sheaf of wheat representing Ohio's agricultural strength and a bundle of seventeen arrows shows Ohio to be the 17th state to enter the Union. The mountains and rising sun signify that Ohio was one of the first states west of the Alleghenies. The Scioto River flows between Mount Logan and the cultivated fields in the foreground. The design is said to have been the cooperative inspiration of Thomas Worthington, "Father of Ohio Statehood;" Edward Tiffin, the first governor; and William Creighton, first secretary of state. After an all-night meeting at "Adena," the magnificent estate of Worthington, they viewed the sun rising over Mt. Logan and the hills of what is now Great Seal State Park thus inspiring the scene of the Great Seal of the State of Ohio (Ohio Department of Natural Resources, 2009).

Visitors can not only conquer twenty-three miles of trails (from some of which you can see Columbus on a clear day, according to the park's site), but may also find camping, picnic areas, and recreational activities such as disc golf, horseshoes, paintball, playgrounds, volleyball, and basketball.

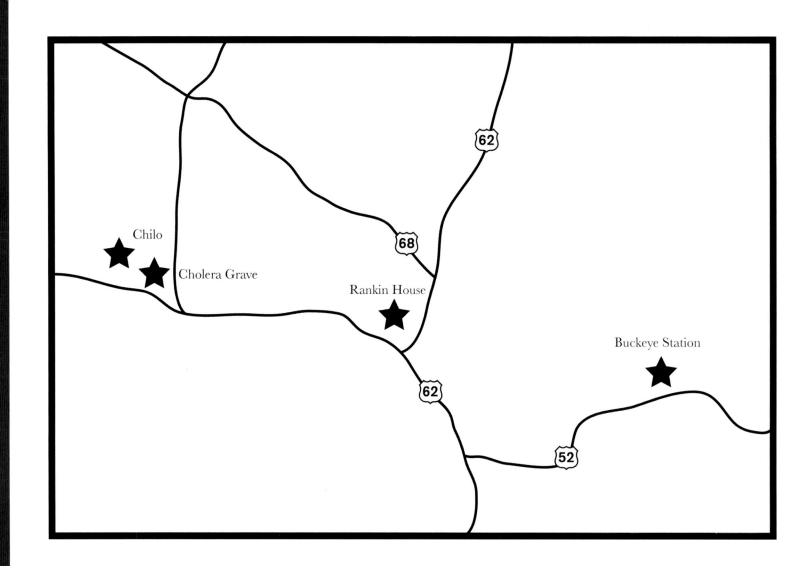

Chilo

Cholera Grave

Rankin House

Buckeye Station

62

68

62

52

Chapter Seventeen

Ohio River Life

If you travel east along the Ohio River, you'll come across sleepy hamlets and small river towns containing the occasional marina and diner. Each has its own personality and special history.

Chilo is one such town with a few worthwhile stops. Surprisingly active for being on such a quiet stretch of Route 52, Chilo Lock #34 Park is a pleasurable way to learn about Ohio River history. Crooked Run and Buckeye Station offer quiet reflection, while the Meldahl Lock and Dam allows visitors to see how important the river is even in our modern, fast-paced world.

Chilo Lock #34 Park

521 County Road, Chilo, OH 45112

- **Phone**: 513-732-2977
- **Hours**: Open daily during daylight hours
- **Cost**: Free
- **Website**: www.parks.clermontcountyohio.gov/Chilo.aspx

There is perhaps no better introduction to Ohio River life than to visit a lock system. Chilo Lock #34 was designed to allow river traffic to pass even when natural levels were down to as little as a few feet while the Meldahl Lock and Dam, located just down the road, was built in the 1960s to replace the aging dam here. Learn more about the importance of locks and dams in the Visitor's Center and Interpretive Museum. For more information on river history, step aboard the replica of a 1800s steamship, the *Jennie Wade*.

While you're visiting, be sure to also visit the Crooked Run Nature Preserve adjacent to the park.

This 77-acre nature preserve is a great location for wildlife viewing. Since it is located miles from any major town or city, it is rarely crowded, affording perfect opportunities for catching a glimpse of any of the 180 bird species spotted here. A hiking trail, river viewing area, wildlife blinds, and areas for bird-watching round out the appeal of this little-known park. If you're looking for a group getaway, consider renting one of the preserve's two yurts.

Chilo Lock
34 Park

Buckeye Station

Along US Route 52, east of Manchester, Ohio

Located east of Manchester on Route 52, a monument resembling a large tombstone can be seen in a small pull off on the side of the road. This commemorates the site of General Nathaniel Massie's home, Buckeye Station. It was known widely as one of the oldest buildings in the state when it still stood. According to Ohio History Central:

Nathaniel Massie was a surveyor and land developer who helped to organize the Virginia Military District in Ohio in the years after the American Revolution.

Massie was born in Goochland County, Virginia in 1763 and

Buckeye Station

came to Kentucky to farm some land owned by his father in 1783. Trained as a surveyor, Massie was responsible for founding some of the earliest communities in the Virginia Military District in the Northwest Territory. In 1790, he surveyed the site of his first settlement, Massie's Station (now known as Manchester) along the Ohio River. He used this town as his base as he moved farther into the region. Commonly, Massie received a portion of the land he surveyed in payment for his work and, as a result, became a large landowner.

While the house is located on private property and not open to the public, this monument, erected in 1933, gives visitors a good idea of the importance of the region and the Ohio River in the growth of the United States.

Cholera Victim's Final Resting Place

US Highway 52, just outside of Chilo

Located along side US Highway 52 near Chilo is the roadside grave of a sixteen-year-old girl who died while on a wagon train headed west. According to most accounts, she died of cholera and was buried here before her family moved on. A small bronze plaque reads:

In Diana's memory there rests here in the quiet beauty of the valley of the Ohio the dust of a young girl. On July 23, 1823 a wagon train creaking toward the west came to a halt close by. When the train moved forward, one of its party had

been left along the trail as a hostage against time. Diana Whitney, sleeping where the morning sun paints with strange scarlets and magic golds the surface of the River, was 16 on that summer day long ago. Diana, daughter of Lemuel and Sarali Whitney — died July 23, 1823 aged 16 years.

Her tombstone is near the plaque and strangers often leave her flowers and small trinkets — she has never been forgotten and hundreds over the years have mourned the young lady in place of the family that was forced to move on.

This is the roadside grave of a Cholera victim.

Ripley and the Rankin House

Off State Route 52
(at northwest edge of Ripley)

- **Phone**: 937-392-1627
- **Hours**: Wednesday through Saturday 10 a.m. to 5 p.m. and Sunday noon to 5 p.m. Seasonal hours; call to confirm.
- **Cost**: OHS Members free, adults $4.00, children 6-12 $2.00, children 5 and under free.
- **Website**: http://ohsweb. ohiohistory.org/places/sw14/index. shtml#hours

The bust of abolitionist John Rankin of Ripley, Ohio, is visible to passersby in Ripley. The monument stands over his grave, just minutes from his house, which was part of the Underground Railroad and can still be visited today.

Unlike the monuments that usually attract my attention, this one is far from subtle and not at all symbolic, but it is still something I always look for when visiting. In fact, my husband and I sometimes take rides out past Ripley and play a game of who can spot Mr. Rankin first.

According to the Ohio Historical Society, John Rankin was a minister and abolitionist who dedicated much of his life to assisting slaves crossing the Ohio River. Decorated to look much as it would have in Rankin's time, the Rankin house is a National Historic Landmark and is open seasonally (May-October) for self-guided tours.

The view from the top of the hill overlooking the river inspires awe and admiration for the human feats of the slaves who made the dangerous crossing across the Ohio and up the hill to a safe hiding place — and also for Rankin, who defied the law in the interest of human rights views that were ahead of his time.

Rankin House

If you are ever passing through this sleepy little river town, I encourage you to stop by the Rankin house. The hours are seasonal and the road up there is long and winding, so plan ahead if you can. After all, there's nothing worse than getting all the way to the top to find it closed! If you enjoy antiques, there are several shops in Ripley and a few places to grab a bite after exploring history.

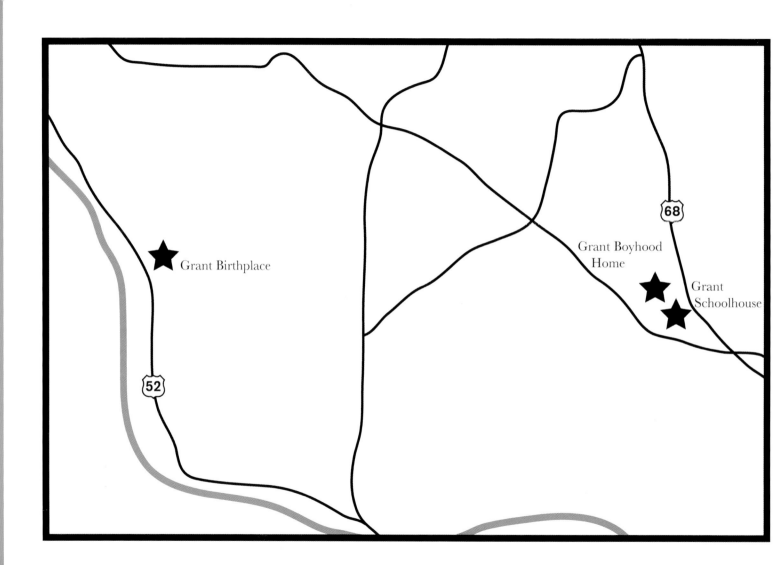

Chapter Eighteen

Grant's Ohio

Grant Birthplace

Born in the Buckeye State? You're in good company. Home to eight presidents, Ohio is a very important birthplace. Logically, then, the state is chock-full of presidential monuments and attractions. President Ulysses S. Grant is a native Ohio son — born, raised, and schooled just a short drive away. The website and contact information for all three sites in this chapter is listed below.

- **Phone**: 800-283-8932
- **Hours**: Wednesday-Saturday, 9:30-5 p.m.; Sundays, 1-5 p.m.
- **Cost**: OHS Members free, Senior Citizens $2.00, Adults $2.50, Children 6-12 $1.50, Children 5 & under free (Covers the Grant Schoolhouse/ Boyhood Home.)
- **Website**: http://ohsweb. ohiohistory.org/places/

The 18th President of the United States, Grant grew up in a house located just an hour from Downtown Cincinnati in Georgetown. Though the Grant family moved to nearby Georgetown when Grant was an infant, the small town has the distinction of producing a president, no matter how short his time in the home there was. The small, white, three-room house is so important that is was once loaded on a railcar and taken on a tour around the United States, as well as displayed at the Ohio State Fairgrounds (site).

Born to a tanner, Hiram Ulysses Grant was born in 1822; the name change came when his sponsor for the United State Military Academy mistakenly called him Ulysses S. Grant, which was shortened to U. S. Grant — and this last one stuck. He served during the American Civil War as a General. He was also a real estate agent, farmer, and tanner (http://www.ohiohistorycentral. org/entry.php?rec=155).

A visit to the Grant Birthplace is an interesting look at some of our most important history. To see the quaint but beautiful home is to truly believe that even those from humble backgrounds can aspire to achieve great things — even obtain the highest office in the United States.

Grant Boyhood Home

This brick house is where Grant spent his life from 1823 until 1839, when he left for West Point. Today, it is set up as a museum where you may view an interpretive exhibit featuring an animatronic figure of a young Grant explaining his life and times. The museum staff is friendly and knowledgeable about Grant's life and the house's history and can even point out the nearby home that once was a tannery. In warmer months, the well-kept grounds are in bloom with native wildflowers.

Grant Boyhood Home

Opposite page: Grant Birthplace

Grant Schoolhouse

The Grant Schoolhouse building was once only one room and was run by John White of North Carolina — and he must have had an impact on Grant, who mentioned the teacher in his memoirs. A small, nondescript building, it is remarkable that a president was educated here during his early years.

Grant Schoolhouse

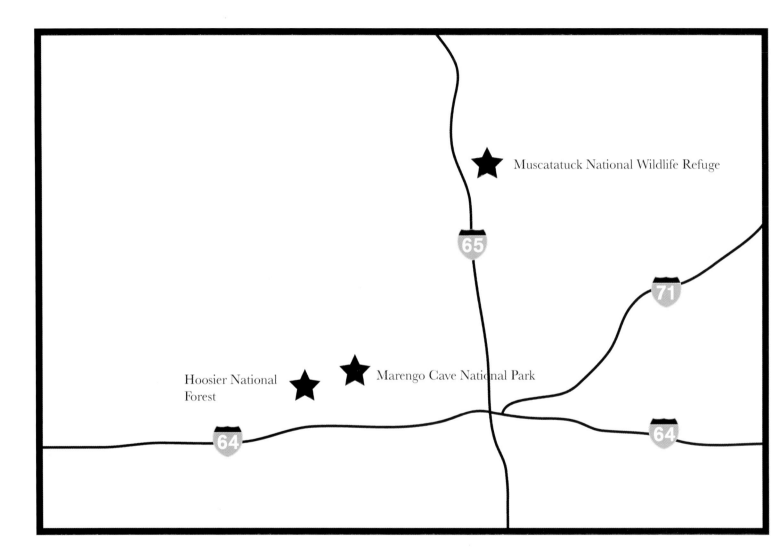

Chapter Nineteen

In and Under Indiana

The Hoosier State offers up incredible recreation opportunities, many of which are not always noticed. Two of the attractions in this chapter — the Marengo Cave and Hoosier National Forest — were planned stops, but one, the Muscatatuck National Wildlife Refuge, was found by chance as we were heading back to Cincinnati. Such is the story of travel in Indiana: there are plenty of well-advertised attractions that are worth your while, but many, many others are happy surprises for visitors who find these hidden treasurers and cannot resist stopping while passing through. The beautiful natural treasures found throughout the Indiana countryside include many caves, expansive parks and plenty of room for exploration. Pack a cooler, grab some comfy shoes, and fill your gas tank — you may find yourself planning one stop in Indiana and end up finding new places to explore.

Marengo Cave

400 East State Road 64
Marengo, IN 47140

- **Phone**: 888-702-2837
- **Hours**: Vary seasonally; call to confirm, especially since it is in an isolated area
- **Cost**: Prices start at $7.00 for children and $13.00 for adults; children 3 and under, free
- **Website**: www.marengocave. com

Marengo Cave is an impressive system of rooms and tunnels chock full of fascinating cave formations such as cave bacon, flowstone, and soda straws. A constant 52.1 degrees, visiting is a refreshing retreat in the heat of summer and a welcome refuge from the bitter cold of winter. This cave boasts a plethora of wildlife, especially bats, making this a fun and educational experience for young and old alike.

Two different tours are available; the Crystal Palace tour, which takes forty minutes and features a beautiful room that inspired the tour's name, and the Dripstone Trail tour, which takes seventy minutes and showcases several historic features such as a square dance area and underground church. The Crystal Palace tour seems to be better suited for children since it is shorter, while history buffs might like the Dripstone Trail, but if you can't choose, a combination pack is available.

Explorer tours for groups are available from $19 to $49 and cover a variety of experiences not found on the normal tours. These are excellent for scout groups and birthday parties.

Kids who are interested in caving, but are too young for an Explorer tour, can still experience the world of a spelunker in the cave simulator called "The Crawler," a wooden model of features found in real caves.

Take your camera (and SLR if you're handy as it will take better photos in the cave), comfortable walking shoes, a change of socks and shoes if possible (caves are wet!), bags and baby carriers that are not backpacks (backpacks not permitted in cave).

This cave was discovered September 6, 1883 by a fifteen-year-old girl, Blanche Hiestand, who heard rumors of a sinkhole near the Marengo Academy, where she was employed as a cook. She was brave enough to beat the schoolboys to the punch and explore the cave by candlelight with her eleven-year old brother Orris. Even more impressive in an age when girls came second to boys, Blanche went in before Orris, likely making her the first person ever to set foot in the cave.

Marengo Cave

Hoosier National Forest

Supervisors Office and Brownstown Ranger District, 811 Constitution Avenue, Bedford, IN 47421

- **Directions**: Call for directions to specific forest areas
- **Phone**: 866-302-4173; Federal Relay System for Deaf and Hearing Impaired Callers: 812-275-5987
- **Hours**: Park open daily during daylight hours; the office, weekdays 8 a.m. to 4:30 p.m.
- **Cost**: Free
- **Website**: http://www.fs.fed.us/r9/hoosier/

This 200,000-acre forest boasts twenty-six miles of trails, camping and picnic areas, boat docks, and rock climbing. Nature enthusiasts will appreciate specimen rules in the forest; visitors may carefully collect nuts, berries, edible mushrooms, and some geological items. Those wishing to collect items or who have questions about what is permitted are encouraged to contact the park office. It must be noted that Native American and historical artifacts are protected by law and may not be disturbed or collected without permission.

If you're willing to follow a few rules, this expansive forest holds many enjoyable treasures and is perfect for everyone from families with children to serious outdoorsmen and women.

Hoosier National Forest is located about two and a half hours from Cincinnati. It's a great general-purpose park for families, boaters, campers, hikers, climbers, horseback riders, fishermen, and hunters. A variety of picnic shelters, trails, and even free camping areas make for a great spur-of-the moment weekend trip when funds are low.

Make sure you grab the sunscreen, insect repellent, nature identification book, and some amateur panning equipment — you can pan for precious stones and gold in some areas! According to the park's website, gold, sapphires, and garnet can be discovered in small quantities. Prospectors may pan for these items as long as no professional equipment is used. Panning is not allowed in the Charles C. Deam Wilderness area of the park; please see the visitor's center for further rules and regulations.

Geodes, a rock hound treat, can be found in creek beds in the northern areas of the park. Collection for personal use is allowed as long as you do not dig or otherwise disturb the soil.

Opposite page: Hoosier National Forest

Muscatatuck National Wildlife Refuge

12985 E. US Highway 50, Seymour, IN 47274

- **Phone**: 812-522-4352
- **Hours**: Open daily
- **Cost**: Free
- **Website**: http://www.fws.gov/ midwest/muscatatuck/

A Native American word meaning "winding waters," Muscatatuck is host to a variety of animal species that call the grassland, wetland, and forest terrain home.

The refuge may not look like much from the road, but a short drive back to the visitor's center will reveal a world you may be surprised to find along a stretch of Indiana highway. Various brochures are available at the stand in front of the center — make sure to pick up the Auto Tour Drive version for a comfortable initiation into this important 7,724-acre refuge.

A four-mile loop with numbered signs reveals important information about each stop, but be sure to keep an eye out for any of the 280-plus documented species of birds, as well as the Indiana endangered species of harmless copperbelly water snake.

The refuge was established in 1966 by the US Fish and Wildlife Service using funds earned by the sale of Federal duck stamps. It has since been named as a Continentally Important bird area for its place as an important migratory stop.

Because so many species can be found on the grounds, please be

respectful of the wildlife. Fishing and hunting leaflets are available, which outline the rules, regulations, and locations for these activities. In a break from rules found in many other parks, edible mushrooms and plants, as well as shed deer antlers, are allowed for personal use.

Birders, families with older children, the elderly, hunters, photographers, and classes or scout groups will all find a visit here worthwhile — and don't forget your binoculars, bird guide (you may also purchase one in the visitor's center), comfortable shoes or galoshes, and a full tank of gas for the auto tour.

Keep your *eye* out for river otters: in 1995, twenty-five river otters, once a plentiful species in Indiana, were released and have thrived since.

Muscatatuck National Wildlife Refuge

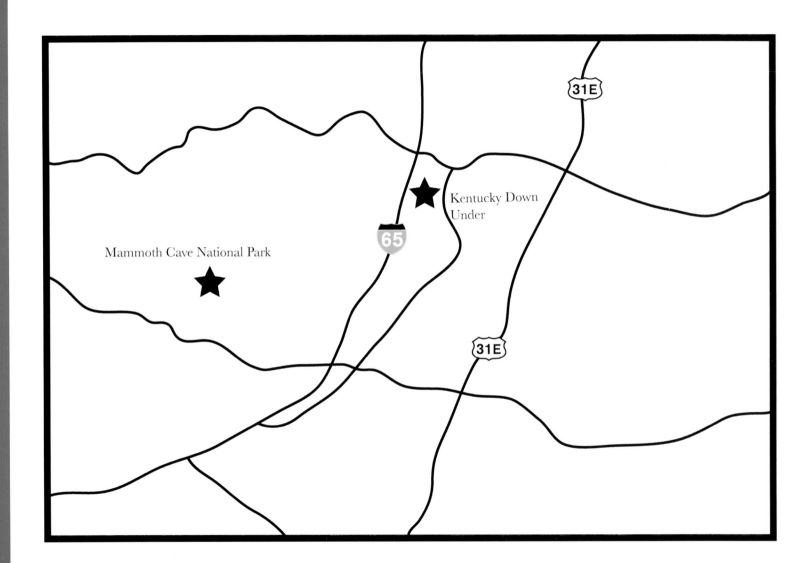

Chapter Twenty

Cave Country Kentucky

Cave City, Kentucky, is the kind of fun you'd expect from a roadside tourist attraction town — and a whole lot more. For every gimmick in this area, there is an earnest landmark or other piece of history; much of this history relies on the brave, entrepreneurial, and sometimes just downright stubborn people who grew Cave City into what you see today. The mix of old and new is interesting — you will find 50's-style roadside attractions and old-fashioned souvenir stands next to modern hotels and chain restaurants. For every dollar you have in your pocket, someone else in Cave City has a plan for it. The good news is that many of those plans are worth the price.

A discussion of Cave City would not be complete without mentioning the story of Floyd Collins, a man who started his caving career at age six and whose life ended in a tragic tunnel collapse. The unfortunate Mr. Collins was trapped as hundreds flocked to the Sand Cave attraction. Most media circuses today would pale in comparison to the coverage and spectacle in the time period rescue operations that took place. Even after his death, he was victim to curiosity seekers who disturbed his grave or slipped tour guides money to see into his glass-topped coffin.

It is this spirit — a mix of true passion for the beautiful natural caves and the desire to attract as many people as possible using the largest gimmicks imaginable — that still exists in this region and makes it such an interesting day or weekend trip.

Mammoth Cave National Park

Mammoth Cave, KY, 42259

- **Phone**: 877-444-6777
- **Hours**: Contact for information
- **Cost**: The park is free; cave tour prices begin at $5.00 for adults and $3.50 for children ages 6-12. Children 5 and under free.
- **Website**: http://www.nps.gov/maca

Mammoth Cave National Park is an excellent introduction to our country's National Parks system. Staffed with knowledgeable park rangers and well marked with modern, interpretive signage, this

park is expansive without being overwhelming.

Don't forget to visit Floyd Collins. The smart thing to do is to buy your cave tour tickets first — if it's a fairly busy day, you'll be on a tour later than your purchase time and you'll have an hour or so to kill. Perfect. That leaves you time to visit Collins. Simply turn right out of the main parking lot and you'll see a gate on the left; turn there and keep driving (and watch out for turkeys!) and you'll eventually come across Mammoth Cave Baptist Church. Take a little gift — his grave is covered with them and many cavers stop to ask his blessing and leave an offering before expeditions. Collins's grave is near the front of the cemetery, marked with a tan stone that reads:

TRAPPED IN SAND CAVE,
JAN. 30, 1925.
DISCOVERED CRYSTAL CAVE,
JAN. 18, 1917.
GREATEST CAVE EXPLORER
EVER KNOWN

Several gift shops are available on park property, both in the historic Mammoth Cave Hotel and the Visitor's Center. There are also several sit-down dining options at the Mammoth Cave Hotel and picnic areas in various parts of the park.

Be advised that absolutely no bags of any sort — including diaper and camera bags — are permitted on cave tours unless they contain medical supplies. A sweatshirt or jacket with pockets is advisable not only for the chilly, sometimes damp atmosphere, but also to carry any items that may be needed while on the tour. Posted signs list prohibited items. When in doubt, find a park employee who can assist you with any questions — they are happy to help and can also point out other areas of interest in the park. Remember your walking shoes and extra socks, as well as layers of clothing for the chilly cave.

Kentucky Down Under

**3700 L & N Turnpike Road
Horse Cave, KY 42749**

- **Phone**: 270-786-2634
- **Hours**: Vary seasonally; contact for information
- **Cost**: Adults 15 to 61, $22.00; Children 5 to 14, $13.00; Children under 5 free; Seniors 62 and older, $19.30; Family 4 Packs (2 adults and 2 children), $50.00
- **Website**: www.kdu.com

Kentucky Down Under is located just off I-65 at exit 58 in the town of Horse Cave, a close neighbor of Cave City. This Australian Outback-themed animal park offers interpretive exhibits with a helpful staff whose members happily take questions and educate visitors on the animal residents. So how did this piece of Australia end up in Kentucky?

It all began in the 1960s. According to the Kentucky Down Under site, Bill and Judy Austin met during that time in New Zealand, where they were both working — she as a physical therapist

and he as an engineer. They later married and moved to Bill's native Horse Cave. After becoming manager of Onyx Cave (today Kentucky Caverns), Bill noticed how much visitors liked the animals that roamed the property. Pretty soon, the two found themselves with a buffalo herd and later added the animals native to the country where they first met.

While this is definitely a kid-friendly attraction, people of all ages can learn a thing or two — and who doesn't want to pet a kangaroo? Don't miss the two bird-feeding experiences: guests can enter the two large aviaries and feed the exotic birds, which aren't shy and will make themselves at home on your arm, shoulder, and even head! Take a few dollars for extra feeding tokens that are available at machines just outside the aviaries.

Kentucky Down Under

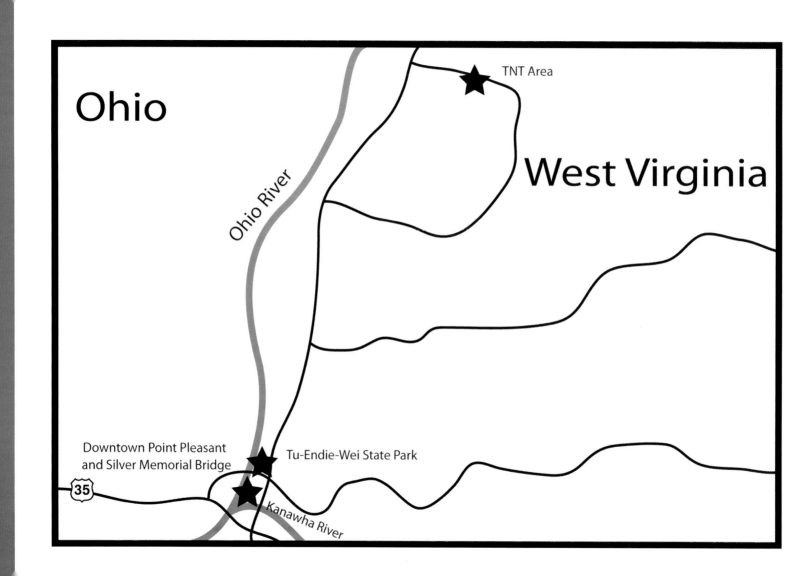

Chapter Twenty-One

Mothman Country

Point Pleasant, West Virginia, is a heck of a lot deeper than most people give it credit for.

With all of the hoopla surrounding the legend of Mothman, not to mention the 2002 film "The Mothman Prophecies," based on the late John Keel's 1975 book of the same name, it's easy to forget that real people experienced real tragedy here with the 1967 collapse of Silver Bridge, which occurred just before Christmas.

Even more, an important Revolutionary War battle was fought in Point Pleasant. The rich and interesting historical sites associated with that battle are often overlooked in favor of the oddities attributed to the Mothman.

When I visited Point Pleasant with my husband, we arrived around 11 a.m. on a Saturday. Feeling a little sheepish, we got out of the car near the Mothman statue to take photos. We felt the eyes of the locals on us as I lined up my shots. Boy, I thought. They must really get sick of gawkers. We must stick out like sore thumbs, but my initial impression was wrong. Not only were there tons of other people posing by various sites and buying armfuls of memorabilia, the townspeople seemed to be eating it up. And why not? I'm sure it brings in a ton of money.

Silver Bridge Collapse Site Memorial

Main Street (near the post office)

Located on Main Street in downtown Point Pleasant, the Silver Bridge Collapse Site Memorial honors the forty-six lives lost in 1967 when a single eyebar with a minute defect failed.

The collapse and subsequent investigation led to stricter bridge maintenance and standards. Today, you may drive across its replacement, the Silver Memorial Bridge.

Aside from the official cause, local legend has it that Mothman sightings

SILVER BRIDGE COLLAPSE

Constructed in 1928, connected Point Pleasant and Kanauga, OH. Name credited to aluminum colored paint used. First eye-bar suspension bridge of its type in US. Rush hour collapse on 15 December 1967, resulted in 31 vehicles falling into river, killing 46 and injuring 9. Failed eye-bar joint and weld identified as cause. Resulted in Congressional passage of national bridge inspection standards in 1968.

Silver Bridge Collapse Site Memorial

in the year leading up to the disaster foretold what would occur. In addition, the sightings cause the town to border on hysteria, leading the townspeople to question their own powers of observation and shake up the sleepy little town.

The Statue

Main Street near The Point

A stainless steel statue of the Mothman as interpreted by West Virginia sculptor Bob Roach stands in Gunn Park, which was rededicated in 2002 as Mothman Park to coincide with the movie release.

The Statue

The Point

330 Main Street,
Point Pleasant, WV 25550

- **Phone**: 304-674-4618
- **Hours**: Contact for hours
- **Website**: www.thepointwv.com

If you want to orient yourself with the Mothman legend, you need to make a stop at a small souvenir shop, almost exactly across the street from the memorial, where we noticed quite a few people congregating. Turns out, we weren't the only ones who were in town to see the sights.

Inside The Point (the name of the shop), we found every sort of trinket from shot glasses to plush Mothmen. As we waited to check out, we heard the owner giving the woman in front of us instructions on how to get to the TNT igloos, which were used during World War II and later became the hotspot for Mothman sightings. We were intrigued, as we had heard they were not accessible

The Point

or open to the public. My husband asked the owner if he had another map, and the nice man proceeded to not only give us the map, but he also gave us detailed instructions for finding the igloos, drew a diagram, told us stories that involved ancient Shawnee burial grounds, and showed us photos taken by other visitors.

TNT Area

McClintic Wildlife Management Area (Ask locally for directions)

Perhaps the best way to describe the oddity of the abandoned TNT igloos is to describe the personal experience I had there.

We located the guardrail the man at The Point had described in his directions. It seemed like we walked forever between a thick, overgrown forest on our right and a foul, stagnant pond to our left. I had gone a few feet too far when my husband called out from behind me, "Hey, I think this is it!"

It was. Through a short, thick tunnel of vines and mud, we found the entrance to the first igloo. It was more bizarre than I expected — and bigger. Much bigger.

The odd thing was, we walked in cautiously, as not to disturb the people inside because, well, we both felt like there were going to be people inside. There weren't.

The man at the store explained that energy travels from one igloo to another and that we should take photos inside. Keeping an open mind, we did that. We saw nothing, but it was still unsettling. The detailed Mothman graffiti and empty black powder cans alluded to the area's past. Everything echoed all around us, from a deep exhale to our footsteps in the dark.

We traveled to the next one, this time down a longer, darker tunnel of foliage. We passed the owners of the cars we had seen in the pull off where we parked, which made us feel a little better. Then we went in. This one made me most uneasy. It seemed to sit back slightly more and it was more overgrown. I felt like if I was going to see anything that day, this was going to be where. I didn't see a thing, but the uneasiness grew.

We found the third one, but didn't linger — it was hot, we were alone in the middle of nowhere, and it was getting weirder by the minute.

We passed the two other igloos quickly, not stopping to take another peek. The pond was making an odd crackling noise; at times sounding like knocks on a door. We felt like there were eyes on us.

We're both logical, rational people and we know very well that there could be cameras around there or even people hiding to play a trick. No matter what gave us that sensation, though, it was enough to give us pause and to make us drive away quickly.

If you're in the mood to stop by the igloos, make the stop at The Point for directions and a map. It's not a good place for small kids and you should be careful of various hazards such as broken glass, snakes, sticker bushes, and poison ivy.

Mothman Museum and Research Center

401 W. Main Street, Point Pleasant, WV 25550

- **Phone**: 304-675-2260
- **Hours**: Open daily, noon to 5 p.m.
- **Cost**: For ages 10 and older, $3.00; under 10 years old, $1.00
- **Website**: www.mothmanmuseum.com

A place that bills itself as the world's only Mothman Museum and Research

Opposite page: The Igloos

Mothman Museum and Research Center

Center is worth a visit. Looking part tourist trap and part souvenir shop from the street, it is home to a surprisingly well-thought out collection of Mothman movie memorabilia, newspaper clippings from the peak time for sightings, and the Silver Bridge Collapse and Mothman merchandise.

Throughout the museum, you'll find props and costumes used in the 2002 film "The Mothman Prophecies," including items used or worn by the film's stars, Richard Gere, Deborah Messing, and Laura Linney. While the Hollywood aspect is surely exciting, the hand-written eyewitness accounts from people who reported sightings of Mothman are chilling and worth the price of admission alone. Don't forget to pick up your free photocopied photo of the late John Keel, located on a brochure rack near the museum's media room where you may view a video on the Mothman phenomena. Make sure to buy a Mothman button or t-shirt on your way out.

Tu-Endie-Wei Point Pleasant Battle Monument State Park

#1 Main Street

- **Directions**: From site: One mile north of junction US 35 and WV 2 or at the intersection of WV routes 62 and 2 in Mason County. The park is just west of this intersection.
- **Phone**: 304-675-0869
- **Cost**: Free
- **Website**: www.tu-endie-weistatepark.com

A very important piece of the Mothman mystery lies only a few minutes from the more modern sites. Tu-Endie-Wei, a Wyandotte phrase meaning "the point between two waters" (West Virginia Division of Natural Resources, 2008), is a slice of land overlooking the Great Kanawha and Ohio rivers. It was

Tu-Endie-Wei Point Pleasant Battle Monument State Park

the location of a bloody struggle — known to some as the first battle of the American Revolution — on October 10, 1774. Settlers and American Indian Tribes had been clashing over land and these fights were becoming more violent. To further complicate things, the British were attempting to align with the tribes in an effort to profit from the fur trade. Lord Dunmore, the appointed governor of Virginia (which at this time was a much larger state that enveloped what is now West Virginia), organized a militia, led by Colonel Andrew Lewis, to protect American land claims. What happened next influenced an epic daylong battle that ended with many casualties and years after the battle, a rumored curse that was carried out long after many had forgotten what happened at the edge of town.

Dunmore sprang into action, hoping to have the upper hand against the Shawnee and Mingo tribes. Peace treaties were signed "with the Delaware and Six Nations of Iroquois at Pittsburgh. He then started down the Ohio to give battle to the fierce Shawnee" (brochure). As Lewis marched his troops to begin battle, his attack was thwarted when Shawnee Chief Cornstalk moved his men and attacked when the militia troops were still converging. The forces met on the Tu-Endie-Wei, engaging in all-day hand-to-hand combat. Ultimately, the settlers prevailed, losing fifty men to the 230 tribesmen. After the battle, Cornstalk sought peace with the settlers who had defeated him. In 1777, the British were trying to side with Chief Cornstalk's men. He traveled to Point Pleasant to tell the Virginians of the plan. Instead of thanking him, the settlers took Chief Cornstalk and two of his men as hostages. What happened next is often called a "dark spot" in American history:

A month later, Cornstalk's son, Ellinipsico, came to the fort to see his father. During his visit, a soldier walking near the fort was killed by an Indian and other soldiers rushed to Cornstalk's quarters to kill him in revenge.

Cornstalk, who is described by historians as a handsome, intelligent, and highly honorable man, stood calmly in the doorway to his room and faced his slayers.

He was felled by nearly a dozen rifle shots. The soldiers then entered the room and killed Cornstalk's son and two companions.

The murder of their chieftain turned the Shawnees from a neutral people into the most implacable warriors who raided Virginia settlements for twenty years after the incident (*Charleston Gazette*).

According to legend, the dying Cornstalk cursed the settlers for two hundred years. Many blame the Mothman sightings and the Silver Bridge Collapse on this curse. Today, the park contains a large monument to the Shawnee Chief, who was laid to rest for a third and final time on park grounds on September 21, 1954. The Chief's only remains are three teeth and fifteen shards of bone. They were put into a metal box and are sealed inside the obelisk monument.

The article written on the day of his final interment details the long journey to his final resting place:

> After his death in 1777, he was buried near Fort Randolph the Colonial outpost at which he had been killed. Then in 1840, street-builders here unearthed his grave, and the remains were moved to the courthouse grounds.
>
> This year, with the decision to raze Mason County's old courthouse and erect a new $700,000 structure in its place, it was decided to move the grave to historical Tu-Endie-Wei Park at the junction of Ohio and Kanawha Rivers.
>
> Amateur archeologists began digging last Saturday morning, and after ten hours of fruitless labor, it was feared that the chief's remains might not be found. But early Sunday, persistent diggers came upon rust stains from the metal box in which Cornstalk had been reburied. In loose earth, they found the teeth and bone fragments, which were decided to be "undoubtedly those of Cornstalk."
>
> The reburial today was directed by members of the Pt. Pleasant chapter of the Daughters of the American Revolution. The story of Cornstalk's seizure and murder is one of the dark spots in American history (*Charleston Gazette*, 1954).

The Cornstalk and Lewis Statues

In a twist of fate that some would call ironic, Chief Cornstalk, General Andrew Lewis, and the Mothman share a bond in stainless steel.

Bob Roach created the Mothman sculpture, which is in view of the Silver Bridge collapse site. Just steps away at Riverfront Park, Chief Cornstalk and General Lewis stand side-by-side as sculptures created in the same style.

The distinct statues gleam in the sunlight, standing in front of yet-to-be-finished murals, some depicting the Battle of Point Pleasant.

Chief Cornstalk
Statue

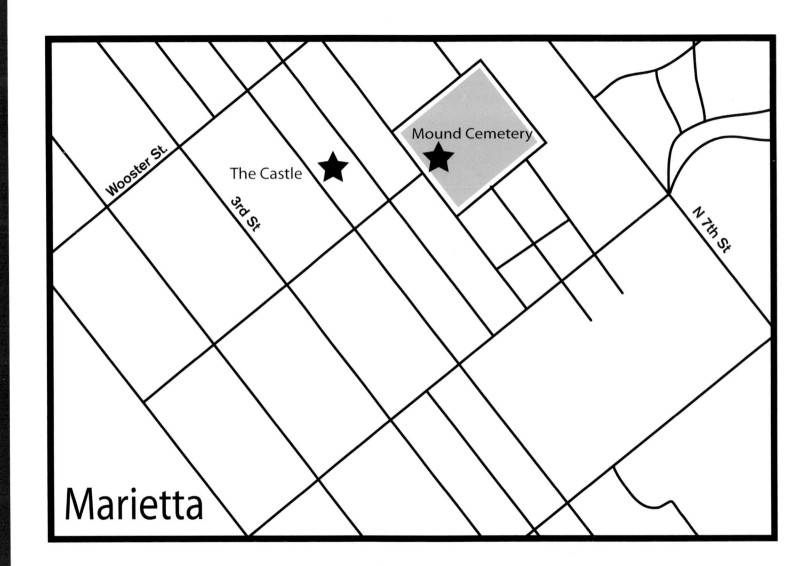

Chapter Twenty-Two

Marietta

This picturesque town is famous for its beginning — in 1788 it became the first permanent settlement in the Northwest Territory. Named after Marie Antoinette, it is home to Marietta College, a lovely shopping and dining district with beautifully restored houses. It's the perfect destination for relaxation, leisurely walks, and learning about Ohio's rich history.

Driving through the older parts of the city, it's easy to fall in love. Large, established trees shade regal old homes. Sidewalks stretch past beautiful churches and through campus. Small parks dot the landscape, echoing with children's laughter and the occasional barking dog. It's idyllic and refreshing, but also a little dark in the way of many towns with history that stretches through tumultuous times. One must wonder about the history of the houses and the times they've stood witness to.

While it's a hefty drive of almost four hours from Cincinnati, there is a lot to do once you're there. There are plenty of little pubs and cafes for leisurely meals and the unique shops would be great for Christmas shopping or just some retail therapy year-round. If you'd like to unwind at a slow pace, The Valley Gem Sternwheeler offers daily river cruises — a great way to see Marietta and surrounding areas.

The Mound Cemetery

5th and Scammel Streets

If you love cemeteries — the ambiance, history, and beauty — you'll adore Mound Cemetery, which can be entered on Fifth Street through a pedestrian gate.

Whereas most cemeteries are arranged in neat little rows, this cemetery is laid out around an enormous Hopewell mound, which is surrounded by a wide, shallow trench. To protect the mound, strict rules apply to its ascent — visitors must stay on the steps, which are a somewhat steep but manageable trip. At the top, they will find a few benches to take in the view and plaque

commemorating something I'll leave as a surprise to those who reach its summit.

Among the graves located is Marietta founder Rufus Putnam. The older stones are fascinating and beautifully carved. It is possible to spend quite a long time here, enjoying the scenery.

The Castle

418 Fourth Street
Marietta, OH 45750

- **Phone**: 740-373-4180
- **Hours**: April 1 to May 31 and September 1 to December 31, Thursday to Monday; June 1 to August 31, daily. Weekdays hours: 10-4 p.m.; weekends, 1-4 p.m.
- **Cost**: Adults, $6.00; seniors, $5.50; students ages 6-17, $3.
- **Website**: www.mariettacastle. org

This beautiful nineteenth century Gothic Revival home/castle is a fine example of the exquisite architecture found in historic Marietta. It is open for tours and occasionally hosts art exhibits.

Opposite page: The Mound Cemetery

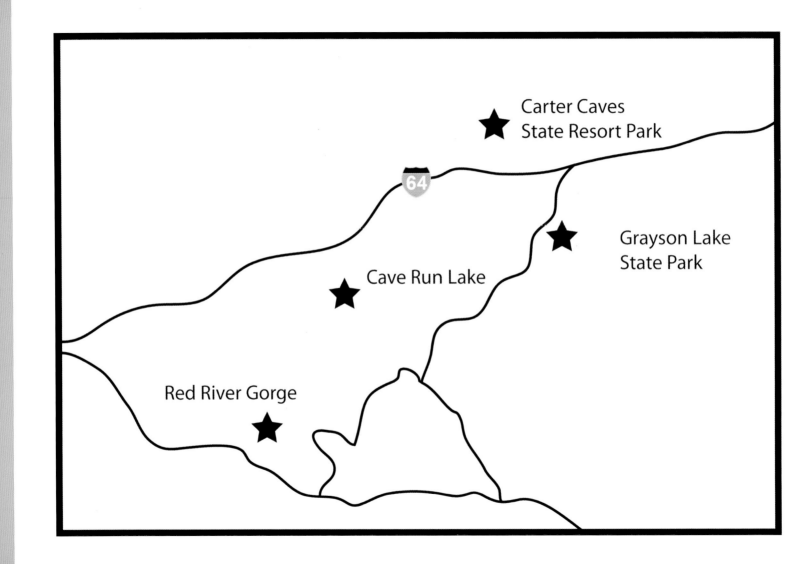

Chapter Twenty-Three

Gorgeous Gorges

Heading deep into Kentucky to the Daniel Boone National Forest is almost like being in another country. Impressive rock formations and beautiful sweeping views can be found on the side of road, not even marked as points of interest on any map. Punctuated by truck stops and small towns, the way from Cincinnati to the following attraction is long and meandering, but definitely worthwhile.

Red River Gorge, Cave Run, and Grayson Lake command respect and, while all ages and ability levels can enjoy them, there are areas best left to experienced hikers, campers, and climbers. A stop at the parks' ranger stations can help you get oriented and find the best areas to explore. For all of these parks, you should be equipped with the proper shoes and a change of clothing if you plan to do much hiking. It doesn't hurt to play it by ear and throw your tent in the car — if you like what you see, just get a permit and stay the night.

Red River Gorge

3451 Sky Bridge Road, Stanton, KY 40380

- **Phone**: 606-663-8100
- **Hours**: Daylight hours
- **Cost**: Free
- **Website**: http://www.fs.fed.us/ r8/boone/districts/cumberland/ redriver_gorge.shtml

Located just over two hours from Cincinnati, the Red River Gorge Geological Area is a Mecca for climbers, primitive campers, hardcore hikers, and college kids looking for a distraction from their studies. A strange mix of locals, amateur outdoorsmen, and expert climbers, the towns of Stanton, Slade, and Rogers see an influx of visitors every spring that lasts long into the fall — when one last hurrah comes with peak autumn color.

Most family-friendly activities are clustered around the Natural Bridge area. A sky lift with gift shop is a good option for those with children, as the hike to the top can be strenuous, especially in the summer months. In the area around Hemlock Lodge and Hoedown Island, playgrounds, miniature golf, and other kid-friendly distractions can be found.

In more remote areas of the park, you will find college kids and experienced outdoor enthusiasts who primitive camp in designated areas. One of the most popular meeting places for these groups is Miguel's Pizza and Rock Climbing, which is located at 1890 Natural Bridge Road. If you're a climber, a stop here is a must.

Make sure to make a pass through the famous Nada Tunnel, which dates back to 1910 and was completed two years later, and was originally used as a pass to haul timber. You may have to wait a while for your turn, as it's one-lane and very popular.

Red River Gorge

Cave Run

150 State Highway 826
Morehead, KY 40351-9211

- **Phone**: 606-784-9709
- **Hours**: Daylight hours
- **Cost**: Free

Cave Run Lake, which comes in at over 8,000 acres, is a haven for boaters and fishers. Even people wary of lake swimming will enthusiastically join in due to the clear, clean water — often an adult can wade from the beach to waist-deep water and still see his or her feet and the occasional fish.

Miles of fire roads are the delight of those with four-wheel drive, many of which take drivers to fantastic views and such far-flung areas of the park that it's easy to imagine you're all alone.

A beautiful campground, primitive camping areas, and local cabins and hotels give visitors plenty of options should they decide to stay for more than one day. Since the town of Morehead is nearby,

you can find modern conveniences when you need them and still retreat back to the park to continue your adventure.

The Minor Clark Fish Hatchery, located at 120 Fish Hatchery Road and owned by the state of Kentucky, is a great destination for people of all ages. A large concrete pool allows visitors to view many native fish species in clear water. Signs help with identification of species.

Cave Run

Grayson Lake

314 Grayson Lake Park Road
Olive Hill, KY 41164-921

- **Phone**: 606-474-9727
- **Website**: www.parks.ky.gov

Grayson Lake is often forgotten for the more popular Red River Gorge and Cave Run State Park, but its unique features make it a must for any outdoor lover's itinerary.

Popular with boaters, kayakers, and canoeists, this 1,512-acre park offers spectacular paddling that will take you past impressive cliff faces and small caves and into shaded coves. If you're lucky, you may even see a freshwater jellyfish, as I did on a canoe trip in 2007.

The 71-site campground is a three-hour journey from Cincinnati, but modern and family-friendly with nice shower houses and restrooms. In addition, Hidden Cove Golf Course, picnic areas, playgrounds, a public beach, and hiking trails all offer plenty of recreational activities.

Grayson Lake

Carter Caves State Resort Park

344 Caveland Drive, Olive Hill, KY 41164-9032

- **Phone**: 606-286-4411
- **Hours**: Tours vary by season; contact for more information. Park open during daylight hours.
- **Cost**: Tour costs begin at $7.00 for adults and $4.00 for children
- **Website**: http://www.parks. ky.gov/findparks/resortparks/cc/

If you're looking for an all-inclusive day-trip or weekend getaway, Carter Caves State Resort Park is the ideal destination. Boasting Lewis Caveland Lodge and cottages, eighty-nine campsites, and group camp buildings, there are plenty of accommodation options should you extend your stay for a whole weekend — and why wouldn't you want to?

You can take a break from exploring the park and eat at Tierney's Cavern Restaurant, which serves local meat and produce whenever possible. Visitors can also enjoy the 45-acre Smokey Lake via guided canoe tour, which is $10 for adults and children age 13 and up and $5 for children (available seasonally; sign up at the Welcome Center). A golf course, hiking and horseback riding trails, swimming pool, miniature golf, and tennis courts round out the family-friendly activities offered at the park —

and I haven't even mentioned the main attraction!

The park's namesake, Carter Caves, refers to Kentucky's largest concentration of underground tunnels and caverns. Tours are operated year-round in two of the caves in this system: Cascade and X-Cave. A third cave may be explored independently with the proper permit, available at the Welcome Center. According to the park's website:

"X Cave is filled with beautiful and strange forms. Stalactites and stalagmites are found along the right passage of the cave. Columns, draperies, and flowstone created by centuries of water percolating through earth and stone, decorate portions of the cavern." Another curiosity is "Pipe Organ." This formation is unique in that several stalactites and draperies, when struck with a piece of wood, sound different tones, thus giving it its musical instrument name" (Kentucky State Parks, 2009).

Cascade Cave, according to the site, is:

"... filled with dripstone formations of different types. The entrance to Cascade Cave is located on the side of one of the many sinkholes in the area. Highlights of the cavern include, 'Counterfeiter's Room' named for the supposed use of the cave by counterfeiters. The 'Lake Room,' so-called for the large pool of water located there...Cascade Cave also has a beautiful 30-foot underground waterfall" (Kentucky State Parks, 2009).

As with other caves mentioned in this guide, you'll need sturdy shoes, clothing layers, and extra socks in case your feet get wet while on a tour. It doesn't hurt to take your swimsuit and maybe an overnight bag — there is lots to do at this resort and night can creep up before you know it while you're having fun.

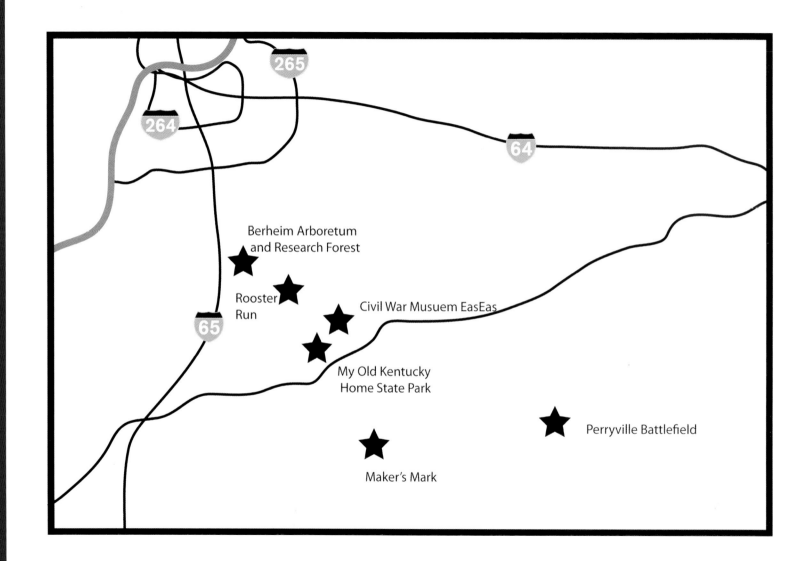

Chapter Twenty-Four

Bourbon Country

Bardstown, Kentucky, and its surrounding areas are so jammed-packed with history and heritage, you might head there for a day-trip and decide to stay for a weekend or more.

While you'd be hard-pressed to visit every destination in this chapter in one day, if you're willing to head out early, come back late, and do a little planning, you can certainly pack two or three places into a long day. However, Bardstown is best enjoyed at a leisurely pace, so consider a longer stay if you have the time.

In this area, you'll find bourbon distilleries, Civil War stops, and southern hospitality at every turn.

Bardstown

If you're looking for somewhere with a slower pace than a big city and not as touristy as, say, Gatlinburg, Bardstown will satisfy your need. Slow and welcoming, yet exciting and stimulating, this little town packs a lot of punch — which just might be spiked with Maker's Mark, as the distillery is located just a short drive away.

Many visitors find themselves in town to visit My Old Kentucky Home State Park, where they can see "Stephen Foster: The Musical."

Old Talbott's Tavern is a well-loved restaurant with a colorful history. Known as the oldest Western stagecoach stop in the country, it has played host to several illustrious and/or infamous patrons.

From its website:

According to legend, figures straight from the history books sought lodging here during their travels; as a young boy Abraham Lincoln and his family stayed here, Gen. George Rogers Clark, Daniel Boone, and exiled French King Louis Phillipe and his entourage stayed here, even painting murals on the upstairs walls. There are noticeable bullet holes in the now faded paintings and Jesse James is said to be responsible for them (Talbott's Tavern, 2006).

Today, anyone, famous or not, local or tourist, can enjoy a good old-fashioned meal, cold drinks, and even lodging in six upstairs rooms — the same comfort it gave to weary travelers in its early days.

Maker's Mark

3350 Burks Spring Road Loretto, KY 40037

- **Phone**: 270-865-2099
- **Hours**: Tours are conducted every hour on the half hour, beginning at 10:30 a.m. until 3:30 p.m., Monday through Saturday. Sunday tours run at 1:30, 2:30 and 3:30 p.m. from March to December (no Sunday tours in January or February).
- **Cost**: Free
- **Website**: http://www. makersmark.com/how-its-made/ distillery-tour/index.siv

Maker's Mark

The world-famous red wax-dipped bottles are immediately recognizable, but have you ever wondered where Maker's Mark comes from? Head down to Loretto, Kentucky where you can not only see where this Kentucky straight bourbon whisky is made, but also purchase and dip your very own bottle of Maker's Mark in the gift shop — if you're at least 21, of course. You can also purchase everything from branded shot glasses to candies and fudge made with the famous bourbon.

Civil War Museum of the Western Theater

310 East Broadway, Bardstown, KY 40004

- **Phone**: 502-349-0291
- **Hours**: March 1 to December 15, open daily 10 a.m. to 5 p.m.
- **Cost**: Adults: Civil War Museum, $6.00, Pioneer Village, $4.00, Women's Civil War Museum, $4.00, War Memorial of Mid America Museum, $4.00, Wildlife/Natural History Museum, $4.00. Children (7-12): Each attraction, $2.00, All attractions, $4.00. Children under 7 are free and special group rates available by arrangement.
- **Website**: www.civil-war-museum.org

This comprehensive little museum is housed in what used to serve as Bardstown's waterworks and icehouse building. Containing glass cases of Civil War artifacts ranging from uniforms to artillery, the galleries of this museum often have an eerie effect — this only adds to the quiet, somber and occasionally slightly morbid way with which most towns ravaged by the Civil War all those years ago treat the subject.

While My Old Kentucky Home State Park and Marker's Mark attract the most crowds, small, independent museums such as this offer respite from brutal summer heat and long lines during peak months. In addition, you often get unadulterated information and bare-bones facts that are sometimes obscured by big-name attractions.

This museum is one of five attractions housed under the same management. Special pricing is available if you choose a combination of any three or all five of the attractions.

Perryville Battlefield State Historic Site

1825 Battlefield Road
Perryville, KY 40468

- **Phone**: 859-332-8631
- **Hours**: Daylight hours
- **Cost**: Free
- **Website**: www.parks.ky.gov

It's tough to believe that the peaceful, rolling hills of this State Historic Site were the scene for carnage like nothing the region had never seen. After the last rounds of the Battle of Perryville were fired, 6,000 men were dead, injured, or presumed missing (site). Because of this, October 8, 1862 is commemorated each year with demonstrations.

Sadly, the sheer brutality and aftermath of this battle did not leave time or energy for the proper burial of all dead. Today, near the museum and gift shop, a large stone monument marks the location of a mass grave containing the remains of Confederate soldiers.

According to local legend, so many rounds were fired during the battle that mills would not accept the wood from any tree in the area, as it was so riddled with lead it was unusable.

Perryville Battlefield State Historic Site

Bernheim Arboretum and Research Forest

State Highway 245, Clermont, KY 40110

- **Phone**: 502-955-8512
- **Hours**: Open daily 7 a.m. to sunset; the Art Gallery and Nature Shop open daily, 9 a.m. to 5 p.m. (Both closed Christmas and New Year's Day.)
- **Cost**: $5 per car, minivan, or motorcycle, $10 per passenger van or RV, $20 for buses on Saturday, Sunday, and holidays; Monday-Friday visitors get in free.
- **Website**: www.bernheim.org

Bernheim Arboretum and Research Forest

Perhaps more than any other attraction in this chapter, Bernheim Arboretum and Research Forest epitomizes the beauty and generosity of the region. Isaac W. Bernheim, also known as I. W., was a German immigrant who made his home and whisky fortune in Kentucky. He gave this piece of land to the state as a gift; today, people from all walks of life enjoy the paths, gardens and wildlife at Bernheim.

Beautiful in all seasons, whether you spend a few hours or the entire day, this attraction is well worth the price of admission. Cycling is an excellent way to see the arboretum, so throw your bike on the rack if you're so inclined.

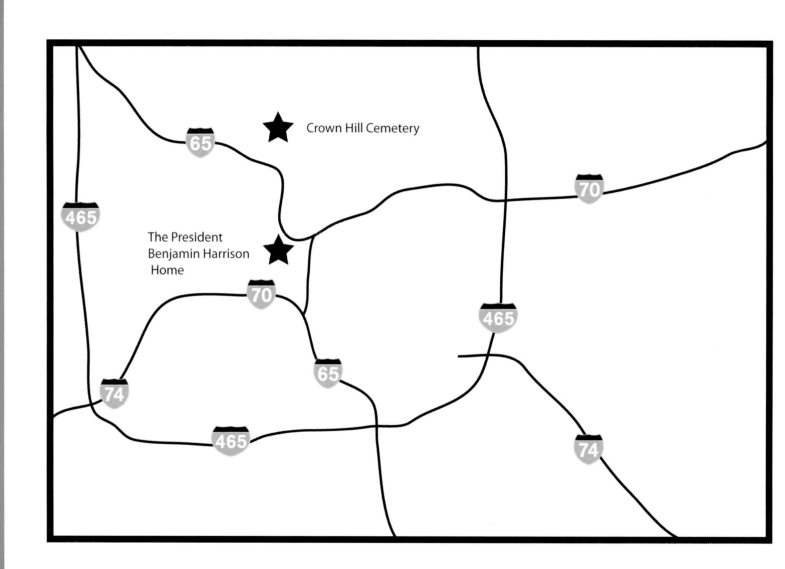

Chapter Twenty-Five

Indianapolis Off the Beaten Path

Our neighbor to the northwest, Indianapolis, is a popular weekend destination for Cincinnatians. A smaller city much like Cincinnati, it's easily navigated by out-of-towners. It's far enough away to make visiting a treat, but close enough to share weather. With its professional basketball, world-champion NFL team, and racing heritage, it's a dynamic city with plenty of diversions.

There is plenty of great shopping and dining at the popular Circle Centre Mall and surrounding areas. The renowned Children's Museum of Indianapolis, which features the largest permanent installation by Dale Chihuly, is a colorful wonderland for kids and adults alike. The Indianapolis Museum of Art features works by such artists as Georgia O'Keefe, Norman Rockwell, and Paul Cézanne and is open to the public free of charge.

With all of these wonderful attractions, it's easy to forget a few lesser-known but important attractions that make great additions to any Indy itinerary.

Crown Hill Cemetery

This cemetery is massive with the brick walls and regal gates giving it an air of importance even before visitors figure out that several notable — and notorious — figures make this their final resting place.

In addition to the notable burials discussed below, Dr. Richard J. Gatling, who invented the gun bearing his name, is buried in Section 3, Lot 9. Indiana poet James Whitcomb Riley is buried in Section 61, Lot 1, and Pulitzer-prize winning author Booth Tarkington in Section 13, Lot 56.

Dillinger's Grave

In most cemeteries, notable burials are often politicians, philanthropists, or local heroes. In this case, it's almost the very opposite — a hardened criminal is one of Crown Hill's most-visited gravesites.

Just calling Dillinger a criminal, however, would be a mistake. He broke the law, yes, but he also became a depression-era folk hero, as he sought revenge on the very same banks that were seizing homes and farms all over the Midwest. In other words, he was playing out the darkest fantasies of many law-abiding citizens.

Dillinger's grave is located in Section 44, Lot 94. A larger family stone is visible from the road.

The 23rd President

Benjamin Harrison was born in North Bend, Ohio, just a half-hour outside of Cincinnati and moved to Indianapolis as a young adult. He served in the Union Army as Brigadier General during the American Civil War. He currently stands as the only president elected from the state of Indiana.

Harrison's Grave

700 West 38th Street
Indianapolis, IN 46208

- **Phone**: 317-925-3800
- **Website**: www.crownhill.org

Harrison's Grave

Opposite page: Dillinger's Grave

Crown Hill Cemetery has the distinction and honor of being the final resting place of our 23rd President, Benjamin Harrison, in Section 13, Lot 57. First Lady Caroline lies next to him in the plot.

Today, a respectable monument stands over the Harrison family plot. A sign is visible from the road within the cemetery and a paved path leads back to the gravesite. Before you visit the cemetery, print a map, which is available online or make a stop at the office located near the entrance. If you're also visiting the Indianapolis Museum of Art, this cemetery is located near the complex.

Harrison Home

1230 North Delaware Street, Indianapolis, IN 46202

- **Phone**: 317-631-1888
- **Hours**: Vary seasonally, so call for more information
- **Cost**: Children under four, free; children 5 to 17, $3.00; Adults 18 to 64, $8.00; seniors 65 and older, $6.00. AAA discounts are available.
- **Website**: www.presidentbenjaminharrison.org

The Harrison men were born for politics. John Scott Harrison, Benjamin's father, served two terms in Congress. His grandfather, William Henry Harrison, was our ninth president —

and Benjamin's namesake was his great-grandfather Benjamin Harrison V, who served as Virginia's governor and signed the Declaration of Independence (Tourism Development Division, Indiana Department of Commerce). It's no surprise, then, that the Harrison home is a stately manse with all the trappings of a fine life — from packed bookshelves to oil paintings to excess fabric pooling at the bottom of drapery (a tour guide pointed out this was a sign of wealth). Each room holds significance not only because a president once used it, but also because each gives a glimpse into what life was like in the late 1800s. From Caroline's paintings to a pot of soup beans boiling on the kitchen stove, a fine attention to detail and preservation means this house looks much as it would have over one hundred years ago.

Harrison Home

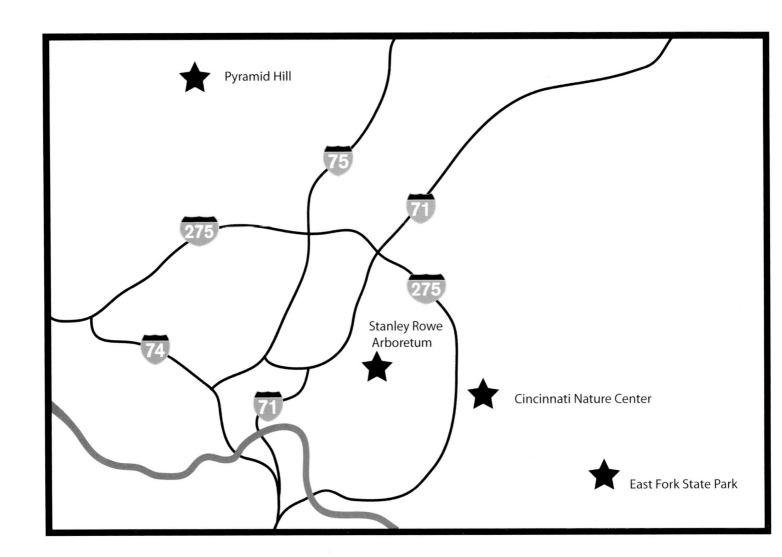

Chapter Twenty-Six:

Closer to Home

The attractions in this chapter are within an hour's drive of downtown Cincinnati. They can be visited for an hour or the entire day, depending on your mood. These locations are perfect for a day with out-of-town guests after you've exhausted all the traditional Cincinnati options—and they are great for letting kids spend some excess energy or taking a peaceful walk or drive. And why not take a picnic lunch?

Kelly Nature Preserve

**297 Center Street (SR 126)
Loveland, OH 45140**

- **Hours**: Daylight hours
- **Cost**: Free
- **Website**:
http://parks.clermontcountyohio.gov/Kelley.aspx

This 42-acre nature preserve is located no more than a half hour from downtown Cincinnati and is well-known among paddle sport lovers as it is an excellent place to put in on the Little Miami, with a nice current and sandbars that pose a little challenge. There are hiking trails, which take visitors through a prairie active with wildlife such as deer, hawks, and songbirds, as well as native wildflowers.

Kelly Nature Preserve

Cincinnati Nature Center

4949 Tealtown Road
Milford, OH 45150

- **Phone**: 513-831-1711
- **Hours**: Vary seasonally; call ahead for hours
- **Website**: www.cincynature.org

Like Shawnee State University, the Cincinnati Nature Center in Milford is dear to me. My husband and I were married at Krippendorf Lodge in this park in 2006. When we were choosing a site for our wedding, it was the first place that came to both our minds. And why not? We had spent countless hours at this well-kept park just outside of Milford hiking, bird watching, and even taking walks in the new snow during the winter just to get out of the house.

Located just a half hour from Cincinnati, the Nature Center is popular

Opposite page: Krippendorf Lodge at the Cincinnati Nature Center.

with many locals who enjoy the lake boardwalk, where turtles can be seen swimming in the clear water, and the Visitor's Center, with its charming gift shop and interpretive displays, and the miles of trails through scenic woods.

Many visitors enjoy photographing and exploring the well-loved Krippendorf Lodge, a home built by Carl Krippendorf, whose father owned the Krippendorf-Dittman shoe company in Downtown Cincinnati (a building which today houses Sycamore Place Lofts). Carl was ill as a child and advised to spend time taking in fresh air in the country, so he grew to love the outdoors and eventually built the lodge for his wife Mary. Today it can be visited from the outside or rented for private functions.

Cincinnati Nature Center is truly a place for all seasons, as many of the trails can be used with care in most weather. In the summer it can be busy with families taking nature walks, and in the winter the solitude welcomes photographers and dog owners who brave the cold to shake off cabin fever.

East Fork State Park

3294 Elklick Road
Bethel, OH 45106

- **Phone**: 513-734-4323
- **Website**: http://www.dnr.state.oh.us/parks/eastfork/tabid/732/Default.aspx

If you're looking for a place to launch your boat, kayak, or canoe, East Fork State Park, located just forty minutes from Downtown Cincinnati in Clermont County, has excellent launch facilities and numerous peaceful coves to explore. The park is also popular with those who enjoy leisurely Sunday drives on the park's nicely paved roads, hikers and mountain bikers who enjoy the miles of well-kept trails, and families who bring picnics and gather for games of softball. The beach is popular in summer months for families wanting to cool off,

and fishermen dot the shores when the first hint of spring comes.

There's plenty at East Fork for history buffs, too. A church and cemetery dating from the early 1800s can be found on Elklick Road — many of the headstones reveal surnames that can still be found in the county today. When I had the rare opportunity to visit inside the church as a Girl Scout, I was shocked to learn that if children misbehaved during Sunday School, the teacher would make them take off their socks and shoes, stick their feet outside, and warn them that a snake could bite their toes at any time. I guess that's one way to keep kids in line. Whether that's true or not, I'll never know, but it's an interesting story. In addition to the historic church and cemetery, there are traces of a short-lived but feverish industry. In the late 1869s, small gold mining operations were present in the Elklick and Twin Bridges areas. Evidence of those mines can still be found today.

Opposite page: East Fork State Park

Stanley Rowe Arboretum

**4600 Muchmore Road
Indian Hill, OH 45243**

- **Phone**: 513-561-5151
- **Hours**: Daylight hours
- **Cost**: Free
- **Website**: http://www.ci.indian-hill.oh.us/departments/rowe.html

Muchmore Road is a popular shortcut for those headed to the Kenwood area from Mariemont and surrounding neighborhoods. If you've taken that road, you've passed a sign that reads "Rowe Arboretum." Like me, you may have ignored it for years, thinking it is simply part of a private estate — after all, there are beautiful homes located all along the road and some sit on large pieces of land. Do yourself a favor and take that turn by the sign and visit what is truly a hidden gem.

Founded in 1926 by Stanley M. Rowe, Sr. and Dorothy Snowden Rowe, this small arboretum is a specimen garden for conifer lovers. Since those were Mr. Rowe's favorite tree type, as many different species as possible were planted on the diminutive nine acre piece of land. A walking trail provides a pleasurable stroll through the gardens and trees and is perfect for spending an hour or two admiring the collection. Quiet, private, and small, it is a great stop for those who are short on time, but would like to unwind after work or get some quick exercise in before a famous Ohio thunderstorm rolls in.

The arboretum is owned by the City of Indian Hill and relies on private memberships and donations — if you wish to give, a donation box is available onsite.

Stanley Rowe Arboretum

Pyramid Hill

Park: 1763 Hamilton-Cleves Road (State Route 128), Hamilton, Ohio 45013

- **Phone**: 513-887-9514
- **Hours**: Vary seasonally; contact for more information
- **Cost**: Adults, $8.00; children 5-12, $1.50; Children 4 and under, free
- **Website**: www.pyramidhill.org

With over 265 acres of beautiful landscapes, adorned with over 50 fine sculptures, Pyramid Hill can be explored on foot, by car, or by perhaps the most fun option: by "Art Cart" — funky painted golf carts that are available for rental.

A visit to Pyramid Hill is a retreat from the everyday. It's easy to spend all day here — and each season lends its own unique charms to the landscape. In addition to the simple pleasure of viewing art outdoors, the park offers hiking trails, bus tours, an art fair, holiday lights and a brand new Ancient Sculpture Museum, which houses unique pieces of art from important eras.

Make sure to take your camera and some comfortable shoes. The park is best tackled with an Art Cart, but there are some places you'll be tempted to explore on foot.

Pyramid Hill

Conclusion

While it would take a book of many hundreds of pages to cover every interesting attraction within driving distance of Cincinnati, I hope you're inspired enough to hit the road in search of a few I've covered and keep your eyes peeled for many more you're sure to discover along the way.

Some have asked me if I'm bored of these places yet — after all, I've been visiting some of these places since childhood. My answer is an emphatic NO! If I wouldn't go back at least one more time, I didn't recommend it to you in this guide. It takes a certain mindset to appreciate the smallest roadside stop, but if you've purchased this book there's a good chance you have what it takes to enjoy learning about your region and all of its quirks, historical tidbits, secrets and legends.

As you hit the road, I hope you'll spread the word along the way — that Cincinnati is perfectly positioned as a home base for many tiny journeys and a superb place to call home at the end of the day.

I must again thank my husband Neil for accompanying me on many of these trips and taking the wheel while I scribbled notes or programmed our GPS from the passenger seat. We traveled hundreds of miles on countless weekends and stayed in many hotels to scope out the places found in this book. We know many stretches of highway like the backs of our hands.

While we carefully planned our trips, we've also been lost, but have always ended up finding our way and discovering a few places by happy accident. If you should take a wrong turn, don't fret. There's something worthwhile around every bend.

Good luck and happy travels.

Works Cited

Charleston Gazette, The. "Fighting Chief Cornstalk's Remains Laid to Rest Again." Charleston, West Virginia, 1954.

Henderson, Andrew. "Woodland Cemetery Hauntings." *Forgotten Ohio*. June 2009. 14 July 2009 (http://www.forgottenoh.com/Woodland/woodland2.html)

"The Moonville Tunnel," *Forgotten Ohio*. June 12, 2009. (http://www.forgottenoh.com/moonville.html)

Kentucky State Parks. "History of Big Bone Lick State Park." 2009. (http://www.parks.ky.gov/findparks/recparks/bb/history/)

History of Carter Caves State Resort Park. 2009. (http://www.parks.ky.gov/findparks/resortparks/cc/history/)

Perryville Battlefield State Historic Site. 2009. (http://parks.ky.gov/findparks/histparks/pb/)

Loveland Castle. *Chateau Laroche*. October 2008. (http://www.lovelandcastle.com/harry_andrews.html)

National Park Service, U.S. Department of the Interior. *Hopewell Culture National Historical Park* (brochure). Chillicothe, Ohio, 2008.

Ohio Department of Natural Resources. *Lake Hope State Park* (brochure). Columbus, Ohio, 2007.

Great Seal State Park. 2009. (http://www.dnr.state.oh.us/parks/grtseal/tabid/738/Default.asp)

Ohio Historical Society. *Cedar Bog Nature Preserve* (brochure). Urbana, Ohio, 1999.

Sanders, Scott. *Glen Helen—A Human Timeline* (brochure). Yellow Springs, Ohio, 2004.

Sroufe, Judith. Honoring an American Icon that Invokes Memories of Enslavement. 2004. Highland Heights, Kentucky. (http://www.nku.edu/~freedomchronicle/OldSiteArchive/archive/issue4/se_index.php?editorial=honoringanamerican)

Talbott's Tavern. History of the Tavern. 2006. (http://www.talbotts.com/html/history.html)

West Virginia Division of Natural Resources. *Tu-Endie-Wei Point Pleasant Battle Monument* (brochure). Charleston, West Virginia, 2007.

Index